SCOTTI MADISON

IT'S NOT THE DUCK

It's the Walk and the Talk

CONTENTS

CONTENTS

CONTENTS

BONUS STORIES AND LESSONS

CONTENTS

INTRODUCTION

Once Upon A Time...
In A Land Called Arkansas...Far, Far, Away

In June of 2002, Scotti Madison received a phone call from Linda Roseborough of Wal-Mart that changed his life as well as the world of Aflac. That phone call put Aflac on the map. It went something like this, "Scotti, this is Linda. Well, our insurance committee met this morning and I have some good news and some bad news. The good news is that we have selected you and Aflac to provide supplemental insurance to the Wal-Mart Associates. The bad news is: even though we initially thought we might be starting in September of 2003, we need to begin this fall, if that is OK? Is this something Aflac can do?"

"Do? Oh, yes, we can do that", Scotti replied after getting up off the floor.

When he said his "goodbyes" to Linda and expressed his gratitude, Scotti fell face down and cried. He had never known such success, or similar accomplishment in the world of sales. For that matter no one else in the voluntary insurance world had ever known of such a feat. Scotti had just landed the largest employer in the world offering voluntary benefits, in particular cancer insurance—and it all began with a cold call.

As a young boy, for long as he could remember, his father had instilled in him good work habits. His parents had also emphasized the importance of education. He played three sports in high school that led to a dual scholarship at Vanderbilt, playing quarterback on the football team and catcher on the baseball team. It wasn't easy and it required a lot of sacrifice, allowing little room for social activities and requiring a highly efficient use of his time. Graduating at Vanderbilt while playing two sports was not easy!

The hard work ingrained early within him traveled with Scotti to professional baseball and later to his insurance sales career. Looking back, at every spring training in baseball, he was always fighting just to make a team. There were no automatic spots on a professional team. When he walked into training camp, there were no guaranteed contracts, salaries, or positions. It was a "make or break" situation every day you showed up to work.

Only twice in ten years did Scotti make the Big-League team out of Spring Training, once with the Detroit Tigers and later with the Kansas City Royals. The majority of the time he was hustling just to keep a uniform on in the minor leagues for one more season, one more chance. He dreaded the day he would eventually hear the "call" in baseball. It's the announcement that comes over the loudspeaker in the locker room or in the cafeteria, "Would Scotti Madison please report to the front offices." Your release from the team was imminent and your baseball career was over. Thus, he was always in survival mode. Whether you liked it or not, you had to be at your best every day.

Scotti was first licensed in insurance in 1978 when he was still attending Vanderbilt. He continued with American Family while playing minor league baseball since he needed a "real" job while he was chasing his dream of becoming a Major League Baseball player. He wanted to work with Aflac because his father first began his career with American Family Life Assurance Company—the insurance company's name when Scotti was in high school and prior to the late 1990's switch to the acronym "Aflac."

So, he played baseball from mid-February to late fall. After the season, he began selling insurance and most of the time it was about four and a half months with Aflac before Spring Training would start up again. He lived this cycle repeatedly for ten years, chasing the fresh cut grass and well-manicured baseball fields down in Florida, while simultaneously building a future in Nashville business. During those ten dual seasons he qualified for every Aflac convention in just four and a half months. Those off-season periods consisted of ten-hour days selling and three hours a day dedicated to baseball training.

The commission earned in sales helped during those lean paying baseball minor league seasons when he made less than $1200 per month. He worked hard because he truly believed in where he played or what he sold. It had to be honorable, and the dream was bigger than the sacrifice. And then of course he kept it fun … it always had to be fun.

When Scotti started his insurance career, he wanted to be better than the average salesperson. He began to work his "walk and talk" skills, and his success started growing. In 1993, he left the comfort of Nashville, his college hometown, and took a lateral job as a District Sales Coordinator for Aflac in Acworth, Georgia, a suburb of Atlanta. He nearly starved the first two years and scratched a living at best.

In insurance, he loved people and was motivated to help policyholders during their financially difficult times. He soon began to thrive on the inner drive of being the best he could be at treating people right. A pat on the back from a friend was more important to him than trophies or sales award trips. You needed to love what you lived … you sell because you love people, and you play baseball because you love the game.

Scotti did not limit himself to baseball and insurance. Some of his future business endeavors would include partnering with Bo Jackson in a nutritional bar called "Better Bar" and later importing patented products from China into retail stores such as Best Buy, Target, K-Mart and Wal-Mart.

In whatever he ventured to do, Scotti Madison enjoyed the journey and learned to cherish the process. He always challenged the man in the mirror to be his very best. Along the way, he learned some secrets to success, often ignored keys that will open locked doors for you, as well.

—KEN ABRAHAM

New York Times Best Selling Author

FROM THE AUTHOR

IT WAS 2014, while sitting in the audience at the Cobb County, Georgia Chamber of Commerce luncheon meeting, that my concerns came to the forefront. I had watched Aflac for years, place more emphasis on "duck advertising" rather than developing a quality field force of exceptional people. It was during this luncheon that Aflac's Chairman, Dan Amos, brought my fears to the light when he addressed the crowded room of one thousand plus business and community leaders.

Dan was someone I considered a long-standing family friend going as far back as to my high school days when my father worked for him during Dan's early years in Pensacola, Florida. My family knew him as "Danny", and he had even watched me personally play high school sports. Now, some thirty years later, I was the most accomplished sales agent in the history of his company, Aflac, the largest supplemental insurance company in the world.

Prior to the event, I had looked forward to saying "hello" and catching up on some memorable stories in the past. Sometimes hopeful expectations never turn into reality. We never visited as Dan appeared eager to get to his speech. Prompted by the pre-luncheon question, "why is Aflac so successful", Dan Amos began to talk about our company success. For thirty minutes, Aflac's chairman told the interested crowd of business attendees how important the Aflac duck commercial was and how he was personally responsible for choosing the "talking duck" for the Aflac advertising campaign. Dan described it as "a very tough decision at the time".

That day, the famous white duck was given more credit for Aflac's success than our dedicated career salesmen and saleswomen. Dan was partly correct; the Aflac duck is arguably the most famous bird/fowl/animal/fish in advertising history and Aflac's brand is well recognized, a household name. The big question then and still today, is the "duck" commercial or any exceptional brand marketing more valuable to the sale than the salesperson? I would argue that no matter how great your brand name recognition is, someone still must sell your product or service. In this world, nothing happens until a sale is made and no matter what product you're selling, "people buy from people." Even better said, "more people buy from exceptional people."

That's when I decided to write, "It's Not the Duck! It's the 'Walk and Talk'". It's how you "walk and talk", which is the "everything else" that makes the sale happen. I am confident in stating that it is the sales team that drives a company. Think about it? Would you rather have an inferior product and a quality sales team or a quality product and an inferior sales team? Which combination would make more sales? All business planning begins and ends with the sales forecast. If the sales team fails to sell, every other business function is redundant. Therefore, it is difficult to find a more important role in any organization than all the salespeople.

Throughout my entire adult life as a commissioned salesperson, I've been searching for the right angle; the right path; the right qualities that lead to greatness. We all have the potential for greatness when we seek to improve the "walk and the talk" in our lives. It is the way in which you impact others that determines your greatness. It is the "everything else" that distinguishes you from the rest of the pack. In this read, our focus is perfecting the "everything else" in you that sets apart your "walk and talk" in sales from everyone else.

Think about it, it doesn't matter what you're discussing, in some sense you're always selling. Talking to a friend about the movie you saw last week is selling your friend on the idea to go and see it. Talking about your spouse and how wonderful they are is selling your friend on the idea "I made a good marital choice". Talking about the Bible is selling the listener on the idea that God is good all the time. America thrives because of the people that sell something every day of their lives. If you think about it, everyone sells something from the moment you wake up to the time your head hits the pillow. You are either pushing yourself, your agenda, your ideas, your product, your menu, your faith or your family and friends.

The forthcoming fifty-two sales tips, one a week, woven with life stories will help you perform with and for people at your highest level. Keeping score in sales is important, yet I think understanding the concept of winning and fulfilling one's purpose in life lies somewhere in between the "participation trophy" and the "championship trophy". It is the road you travel, the actual journey, which provides the foundation for greatness and encompasses the "walk and the talk".

My desire is for this book to be more than a tool to become an over achiever in sales. This is a book on life skills; how to treat people and what it takes to become a better human being. God made you to become your very best. So, let's begin to take the fork in the road that most people aren't willing to travel; the road less traveled; the road where integrity and character are written on the bottom of your shoes; the road where a conscientious effort is made by you to reach your full potential. Ultimately, it's YOU they are buying. YOU are the face of your company, and YOU must figure out ways to distinguish yourself in sales and service from every other salesperson in your own company, and among your competitors. Let's make a gallant effort to keep you, the salesperson, alive and thriving.

This read took considerable time and it required some professional expertise along with some great advice from a few outstanding friends and an incredible wife. First, Darren Welch did an incredible job on the cover design presenting the story before you ever turn a page. And all the content is brilliantly laid out by Bruce Gore, a "chip off the old block", his dad being the late Gary Gore. Ken Abraham, there may not be a finer person and an exceptional author.

Wayne Baswell, a great person and salesmen himself, yet most importantly, my friend since the 4th grade was so helpful reading the early text and advising. And then Danny Karp was instrumental. Dan, as he now likes to be called, will always be Danny to me, and will always be my good friend since high school. He took so much of his time reviewing and making quality recommendations. Thank you all! Finally, my loving wife, Kim, is such an irreplaceable person in my life and a true heartfelt advisor with an eternal perspective. I love her dearly!

1

You Are Always
Selling Honesty And Integrity

It's "The Walk and The Talk"
that Makes a Difference

Zig Ziglar, one of the greatest motivational speakers of all time once stated, "Honesty and integrity are absolutely essential for success in life… all areas of life. The good news is that anyone can develop both honesty and integrity."

I cannot emphasize enough the importance of always being honest in your conversations with everyone you encounter throughout your sales career. It doesn't take talent to be honest. It doesn't take riches to have integrity. Both traits can be held in poverty or in wealth. Always tell the truth. When you tell the truth all the time, you know exactly what you said the last time you spoke with someone. There will be difficult times, when sales are slow, and you might be tempted to fudge the truth to make it happen. So, you stretch the truth, embellish a situation. You rationalize, "It's not really a lie. It's kind of true. It doesn't hurt anyone. My spin is close enough. I could really use this sale." Experience has taught me that even a little compromise will come back to bite you in the butt one day.

Have you ever worked with someone in sales and everything about him or her is exactly what you want to mirror in your life? They are so honest in their "walk and talk" and there is a great calm and peace about them. For me, one such person was Bob Mason, now ninety-three years old. Bob worked with me in Nashville with Aflac and every person Bob talked to knew that he always placed their interest above his. Bob didn't sell, he educated, he cared, he loved people, he just talked. Bob's character and how he carried himself will impact me, as well as others forever.

What is integrity? It's your name; your reputation. Your integrity is what you have that shadows you wherever you go. It's what you leave behind when you walk out of a conversation. You probably won't stay at one workplace for a lifetime and only your name travels with you when you change jobs. Thus, your reputation is the most important constant in your sales career. Besides, you are not just representing yourself when you sell but, everyone's reputation on your team. You are representing your team, your company, your family. How you conduct yourself in business is a reflection on your parents and grandparents, as well as other family members that came before you and all your heirs that will follow.

When your head and heart are right, then your integrity will fall in line. You should do everything within your power to get to a "yes", but it cannot be at the sacrifice of your reputation. In sales, it hurts when we hear the word "no" after you made your best sales pitch, and your bills go unanswered. But guess what? "no" is what you will hear most of the time, so get used to it. If you are not afraid of a "no", there is a good chance you will always give honest answers in your career.

2

It's Better To Say, "I Don't Know"

WHEN I FIRST started selling insurance, I didn't know "jack squat" about insurance, our company, or our products. When prospective customers would sit across from me and ask me a question I didn't know, I might respond by saying something that might not be totally true ... rambling and fumbling with my words about something close to the truth. I'd say, "Yes, we can do that" or "I think so".

Now why would I respond that way? Because I was afraid if I told someone "no", or provided them an answer that was not a positive response, then they wouldn't buy from me. I assumed if they heard, "I don't know", then they would walk away. I think it's something salespeople internalize all our lives, especially when you are new to sales or even when you are desperate to make a sale. It happens often when presenting a new product or service that is not familiar to you.

One such story occurred in the spring of 2015, when I was with my good friend Ray Melvin. Between the two of us, we had seventy years of sales experience, yet we were presenting our Healthcare Analytics Platform out of MIT for the first time in Macon, Georgia to a bunch of "fox" smart insurance brokers. Although we were highly experienced in sales and quite successful at that point, we were novices in the world of Healthcare Analytics. After several visits to Boston, we were armed with direct knowledge from the head of the Operations Research Center at MIT on the subject matter. It still wasn't enough to make us highly effective and confident.

Our meeting was arranged by our friend David Essary, who at the time was a brilliant and aspiring authority in employee benefits. Along with being a Vanderbilt and Harvard graduate, he was very personable and quite likeable. Little did we know that David would one day become the President of Allstate Health & Benefits. Little did David know that he was about to witness the worst sales presentation possibly ever made in the history of employee benefits, certainly in the world of Data Analytics. It was all because Ray and I failed to say, "I don't know".

To our defense, we were both "rookies" on the subject of Healthcare Data Analytics, and it was probably a little too early for us to present. But we were excited about what we had that would change the industry, so we were eager to get started. You have to get in the water to get wet. We didn't realize we were about to drown.

Everything seemed to be going wrong. Ray forgot his business cards and I mistakenly gave out mine before the meeting. We had nothing relatable to warm up our guests after exhaustive attempts to find some common ground. We couldn't keep the Internet connection working, so the presentation on the laptop went dark every thirty seconds. One man in our audience finally had enough, so he challenged our knowledge right up front, "Tell me, this data analytics out of MIT, is it Quantitative or Qualitative?"

There it was, the dreaded question every sales person fears. Ray and I looked at each other and we had no idea how "quantitative and qualatitive" could be applied to Health Care Data Analytics. We simultaneously went into a panic mode. Ray began to sweat profusely and in a matter of seconds he went into "possum mode". I thought he faked his death and began to slide out of his chair. Seriously, he slipped into quiet shock, almost comatose and just stared at the back wall. I felt as if I were wearing an extra small life jacket and couldn't breathe. At what seemed like an eternity, I stared at the man as the room was getting larger and my audience seemed like they were a hundred yards away. Finally, not knowing how either "quantitative or qualitative" could be applied, I found a breath, recovered, and said, "Well Sir, it actually does both." I had no idea what that meant, even though I somehow provided a correct answer.

After thirty years of sales experience, I still had a hard time saying, "I don't know". That man stared at me like I had three heads and no brain. I quickly gave Ray mouth-to-mouth resuscitation … actually, I shook him, "Ray let's go". Neither one of us remembers much from that sales episode. Stupidity will do that to you. I don't think we even said "goodbye" as we walked out of the room and never looked back.

We were sure those men walked away thinking, "These guys are the dumbest data analytics guys we've ever met". We were so embarrassed we couldn't look David in his eyes. We felt sick for him. Today, it would be a different story and in fact, Ray got a "re-do" three years later in front of the same group. He came across as an expert in the field of Data analytics, which he now was.

How easy it would have been just to say, "Sir, I don't know the answer to your question. Please let me get back with you on that quantitative-qualitative question by the end of the business day." Problem solved!

Maybe the hardest three words to say in sales, yet the most valuable, are, "I don't know". It demonstrates honesty and humility, both attractive attributes when building trust in the sale process. Prospective customers appreciate your integrity and admitting "I don't know, but I will follow back up with you" as your answer, can go a long way in acquiring a customer.

3

Attitude Beats Aptitude Every Time

Do you know what the word "aptitude" means? It is "the natural ability to do something." When I think of the word "aptitude", my friend Bo Jackson comes to mind. Arguably, there is no one who had greater natural athletic ability than Vincent E. Jackson, affectionately known as Bo. He and I first met when we were teammates with the Kansas City Royals. The two-sport athlete is the poster child for the words "athletic talent". He is the greatest athlete in my lifetime, and I was fortunate to play with some good ones ... Kirk Gibson and Allan Trammel with the Detroit Tigers; George Brett with the Kansas City Royals; Eric Davis, Barry Larkin and Paul O'Neil with the Cincinnati Reds. Yet, none of them could match the physical skills that Bo Jackson possessed.

If Bo had just relied on his natural skills in the game, he would have only been "great" in professional baseball and football. Yet, he was "exceptionally great" because his attitude and desire to win, to become great, exceeded his incredible prowess. Sometimes your ability leaves you because you are injured or sick and you're just not feeling up to par in the physical part of your game. Still, you grind it out and play anyway. Your "A" game in aptitude stayed home when you came to the "yard" (slang for ballpark). So, the only constant that can possibly remain is your mental attitude.

Do you remember the NIKE commercial "Bo Knows?" Look it up on Wikipedia. It's the commercial that put both Bo Jackson, the two-star athlete, and NIKE on the map. What Bo had that very few elite athletes with exceptional "aptitude" possess is the exceptional "attitude" to win. His disposition, emotional strength, and mindset kept him exceptional in competition even when his abilities took a day off. Bo refused to fail, and it became even more evident after his fall from sports due to a devastating hip injury; an injury he suffered when running the football for the Oakland Raiders in a divisional playoff game against the Cincinnati Bengals on January 13, 1991.

Because of the crippling injury, Bo was released by the Kansas City Royals March 18, 1991, on what is known in the standard players contract as "7B2", insufficient ability. He signed with the Chicago White Sox 19 days later April 3, 1991. He played in constant pain the season of 1991 and had to quit baseball in Spring Training of the next season. I know because I was there when he fell off the wall and could not be put back together.

It was spring of 1992 when I visited Bo in Sarasota, Florida that his football injury officially caught up with him. I saw him walk off the White Sox field in the middle of an at bat due to the debilitating pain in his hip. During this terrible trial in his life, I was his houseguest at Spring Training. That very night I cooked steaks and baked potatoes for those who came to his rescue, in particular Dr. Jim Andrews. I remember sitting at Bo's dinner table when he was told by Dr. Andrews, "Well your injury is worse than I initially thought. Your hip has gotten the best of you. I've supported your comeback over everyone else and painted a glimmer of hope. You got your contract with NIKE and a contract with the White Sox. My butt is on the line now, so I'll do the talking tomorrow at the press conference. You're going to need a hip replacement."

Sitting across from him in the private of his home, I watched Bo's reaction to Dr. Andrews's despairing words. Bo never complained. His face was calm, even stoic. He never became upset. He never cried foul or said, "Why me. I'm the greatest athlete in the world and it's just not fair." He took what was the worst possible news ending the career of the greatest athlete in the history of our lifetime with dignity. His calm displayed his belief that he would overcome. I watched how my friend rose to a higher level. It was a blessing for me to witness his hope in a better day. He was diagnosed with avascular necrosis and had hip surgery two weeks later.

Bo took that same attitude into his hip replacement surgery on April 5, 1992, and it carried over during his excruciating rehabilitation. His natural ability certainly served him well in his recovery. Yet, it was his attitude that made him even more renown when he finally returned from a hip replacement April 9, 1993, to play a home game at Comiskey Park for the White Sox. It was maybe the most special day in Bo's storied athletic career when he homered in his first at bat against the New York Yankees. It was a long road, but he overcame. Bo's inner drive helped him win the Sporting News Comeback Player of the Year in 1993.

So, all of us, even those with exceptional ability, will have an attitude check during our careers. To be great, to be exceptional, you must have an attitude that will carry you through every trial in your life. Your attitude lasts longer than your aptitude and it is what ultimately defines what others think of you for the rest of your life.

4

You Become What You Call Yourself

ABOUT THE TIME I graduated from high school and began driving from Pensacola, FL to Nashville, TN to attend Vanderbilt University, CB radios became very popular. FYI for millennials; CB stands for "citizen's band" radio, which had a dual purpose in the 70's as both a means for receiving directions and a way to communicate with other drivers. It began as the main communication between truck drivers and then caught fire among regular car drivers in America. The movie "Smoky and The Bandit" with Burt Reynolds, Sally Fields, and Jerry Reed ignited the craze.

Communicating with other CB owners (drivers on the road) happened on about 40 different channels. It was a community cell phone with everyone listening to your conversation. The main purpose was to stay in touch or notify other drivers if a "smoky" (code name for a State Trooper) had radar up ahead catching speeders.

When I first started calling other travelers on the radio, I gave myself the name or handle, "Hard Luck." My first fall on the Vanderbilt Football team was indicative of hard luck since I showed up to my first practice on crutches. So, "Hard Luck" seemed like a good name to call myself when I traveled down the road.

That first year, riding back and forth from Pensacola to Nashville, I couldn't get one person to talk with me on my CB radio. I thought for the longest time that my radio didn't work. "This is Hard Luck, come in", and nobody ever answered me.

Then one day I was driving, and a song came on the FM station by Three Dog Night, "Joy to the World". After the song played, I kept playing one particular verse over and over in my head:

You know I love the ladies
I love to have my fun
I'm a high life flyer and a rainbow rider
And a straight-shooting son-of-a-gun

It was then that I found my new name in the middle of the song. I was now "Rainbow Rider". What an optimistic sounding CB handle! That same day, I ditched the name "Hard Luck" and started calling myself "Rainbow Rider". My once quiet drives soon became a highway filled with answering calls from random drivers. All I had to do was say, "Breaker, breaker, this is Rainbow Rider ... come in."

"Rainbow Rider, we gotcha. How can I help you?"

From that day forward everyone wanted to talk to "Rainbow Rider". It was such an upbeat name. Overnight I became the person drivers on a CB radio between Nashville, TN and Pensacola, FL wanted to talk to. I quickly realized people want to associate with positive folks, not some guy that calls himself "hard luck". We may live in a world where "misery needs comfort", yet people desire deeply to associate their inner self with positive re-enforcement. So, talking on the radio they didn't need a CB Buddy with a name that reminded them of their own personal doldrums and daily problems.

To be successful in sales, you must feed your mind with positive thoughts every day. It's either garbage in … garbage out … or treasures in … treasures out. So, consider what you think about and even more carefully what you call yourself. You will become what you think or what you think of yourself. It may be true that motivation doesn't last. Well neither does taking a shower. That's why you bathe yourself daily, so in turn feed your mind daily with optimistic ideas. How do you do that?

For starters, consider hanging around positive people? Or start reading success stories of people who overcame adversity? Successful people are absorbed in reading motivational books and hanging around other positive friends. My favorite stories are the life stories about people who overcame tremendous hardships. The world is full of people who have faced greater obstacles than you and me, yet they still find a way to overcome. Let their difficult road and motivational story be your inspiration.

You should constantly work at being optimistic. I personally begin the first part of my day reading something positive. It might be a story or life account about people in history that overcame great obstacles. Many of my encouraging stories come from the Old Testament in the Bible and the hardships characters faced. During that "Rainbow Rider" time, I seek guidance, wisdom, courage, and protection for the one day standing before me. I encourage you to do the same. Give up 10 to 15 minutes of your morning sleep to get your mind right, your heart right, and your soul right. It will pay great dividends and deliver the proper perspective and internal drive you need to overcome.

5

You Have To Make It Fun

HAVE YOU EVER sat in front of a salesperson that has a melt down and cries when they hear the word "no"? I had that happen to me once. A sales lady was trying to sell me a copy machine in the 1990's and I didn't need one. The pressure of needing a sale overwhelmed her and once she heard the words, "No thank you", she came unglued. She literally broke down and cried. I never did buy the copier, but we did talk about her finding another profession; something far away from sales that involved security, like puppy's and kittens.

That was an extreme case of "selling out of desperation". Finding yourself in a pressure situation at work could lead to believing you must make a sale or else your world falls apart. A wrong thought process creates undue pressure by focusing on the outcome and not the experience. Selling in a "desperation" mindset is not having fun.

This type of thinking is usually founded totally on the self-induced pressure of desperately needing to make money. A desperate salesperson probably needs money yesterday. You need to hit a sales number to make the income and are up against a timeline feeling the pressure of failing. You must figure out a way to change your mindset and remove the self-pressure to make a sale.

One of my best friends in the entire world is Steve Steinhauer. We have always looked for ways to have fun. There was a time Steve, and I were talking with the employees of a company called Grace and Wylie about Aflac policies. It was a steel fabrication business, and these guys were tough blue-collar workers. After two hours into presentations, Steve and I had each spoke with 12 employees and we each sold all 12 of the guys. Steve whispered, "Hey this last guy just bought everything. That's 12 for 12. What about you?" "Yea, my guy did the same thing. He bought everything like the last 11. This is crazy."

We were giddy as it was the first time either of us that had ever sold 100% of anything. Then we decided hey let's make a bet … the first person that doesn't make a sale between us wins the bet. Here's the game, let's try to not sell the next guy that comes in. The first one who doesn't sell a product wins. We agreed!

We were a little ridiculous and I don't necessarily recommend playing this game. By setting such a pressure free environment of "don't sell", we made it fun. Steve and I completely took away the self-pressure to make a sell. On our next prospect, we both purposely made the worst presentations you possibly could make. But it didn't work. Each one of the employees that entered the room still purchased our products. I was laughing just listening to Steve make his pitch, "Hey you probably don't want this Cancer plan, do you? Five dollars a week is a lot of money. You might be better off spending your money somewhere else."

Since it didn't matter to us if we sold anything or not, guess what? We sold everything. That's the way it works sometimes. When you are relaxed and content with the outcome, you don't appear desperate when making your presentation. Thus, your sales results will be far greater. When those pressure feelings come upon you, train your thoughts to "make it fun" and accept the results. It just might work!

6

"You're Only As Good As the Next Game You Play"

MY FATHER WAS one of the toughest football players ever to play at the University of Georgia. The legendary Auburn football coach, Pat Dye, once told me, "Your Dad is the meanest and toughest man I ever saw play football. I idolized him."

He was right! Charlie Madison was a tough man, quite hard on me and Dad never wanted me to rest on my laurels.

My accomplishments in high school football were in the newspaper every Saturday morning after a Friday night game in Pensacola, FL and often in the papers during the spring for baseball. Like many folks whose name appears in the paper, I tended to like reading favorable newspaper articles. The problem occurs when you believe your press clippings and take them too seriously. Listening to folks tell you how good you are can do more damage than good. Dad had foreseen that my head would soon begin to swell and then my performance would go south.

Looking back at high school, Dad believed scoring touchdowns, making good plays, should be the norm and let's not take yourself too seriously. He approached it in an odd way, but he delivered this message clearly to me. Dad reminded me everyday, "Don't look at the past; don't dwell on the past; don't relive the past, either good or bad. Focus on the next time you play because that's what really matters. It shouldn't matter what you did yesterday; there will be a tomorrow that turns into today. So, what really matters is the next time; the next opportunity; the next game; you're only as good as the next game you play."

This same philosophy works in sales when you are in a slump and are hearing a lot of "no's". You can't dwell on yesterday and you need to learn to forget the bad and move on to the next performance. Forgetting "bad days" in sales might be even more important than remembering "good days". Your failures do not determine your future. Remember, your satisfaction comes from being the best you possibly can be the next time you attempt to make a sell.

7

"You Need Thick Skin And Little Ears"

WHILE PLAYING FOOTBALL at Vanderbilt, my quarterback coach was Coach David Lee. Coach Lee went on to develop the "wild hog" offense at Arkansas and later coached with the Miami Dolphins, Dallas Cowboys, and Cleveland Browns. Besides an excellent coach, he was a man of great character and integrity and was also a coach of deep faith, conviction, and principle.

Coach Lee once gave me some sound advice, "Scotti, to be a great quarterback 'you need thick skin and little ears'. You can't allow the fans or the press or even your friends to negatively influence your performance on the field. Someone is always going to say something unflattering about you. You need to hear very little and what you do hear, don't let it get under your skin." Coach was telling me that I needed to be bigger than any criticism that might come my way since negative comments will one day show up at your door.

Coach Lee's advice could also apply to your sales career, as well. You work with people every day and people are human. Sometimes unfavorable words will be cast your way and it might be hurtful. Often it could be your inner circle of peers that are the ones hurting you the most. The quicker you learn to disregard negative comments and to not take them personally ... the better, the stronger, and the more highly effective person you will become. You can't allow disparaging comments to impact you negatively, especially if they are unfounded. Try to distance your feelings from any damaging remark tossed your way. But, if you happen to hear some criticism and you know it's not true, make sure it doesn't get underneath your skin and poison your heart and mind.

8

"Success Occurs When Opportunity Meets Preparation" —ZIG ZIGLAR

BE PREPARED BEFORE you ever make the first call. Use every tool you have at your discretion to find out everything possible about the company you are calling. It doesn't matter what type of company you're calling or what type of product you're selling, being fully informed is vital whether you walk through a prospect's door or talk with a prospect on the phone.

I look back to my college athletic days and remember all the preparation required before we ever played a football game in the fall. In SEC football at Vanderbilt, it started in January when we returned from Christmas break. We began lifting weights followed by daily conditioning. Next, we had spring football practice; then we would give up our summer, take summer classes where afternoons included running, lifting weights, and tossing footballs practically every day. In August, Fall Practice started with two-a-day practices for a week, then two to three more weeks of game ready conditions before the first game.

Looking at professional baseball, we practiced for forty-five days before opening day and that doesn't include all the off-season work. No one succeeds playing a sport without dedicating himself or herself to preparation. Also, no one in sales can succeed without placing equal emphasis on dedicated preparation.

All this research, head knowledge, and personal sacrifice should occur prior to the opportunity to present your product. You have one chance to make a good impression, so why would you not be overly prepared when the game starts? Be fully prepared before you make the first call. Knowledge is power and it allows you to understand your clients better. Everything you want to know about a company is on their website or found by looking at their leadership on LinkedIn. Be prepared by conducting thorough research on your subject matter or client before you ever decide to pitch them your service or product.

9

"He Practiced Way Too Hard"

ONE SUMMER IN Atlanta we decided to take the kids to a Braves game. The Giants were in town and my old friend and Dodger teammate, Dusty Baker was their manager. Dusty Baker had a storied career and was a 19-year player in the Major Leagues mostly with the Dodgers and Braves. He was now the manager of the San Francisco Giants and would hold a similar role for 30 years with the Cubs, Reds, Nationals and Astros.

We strolled down towards the field as a family, and I saw Dusty walking alongside the first base dugout. I hollered for him and Dusty always gracious, came over to meet my children. Dusty approached Tori and Trent with a smile and a gracious hand out to say hello. His first words, "Let me tell you about your Dad. He practiced way too hard."

I wasn't quite sure what Dusty meant at first. But then I

realized he was complimenting my work ethic. For me, that's as good as it gets when it comes from someone like Dusty recognizing my everyday practice habits. Dusty's comment was especially important to me when I'm trying to teach my children the value of hard work. In sales, it's ok to practice way too hard, also. When you practice hard, nothing but good can come out of it. When you work hard, people will notice it and one day your success will come. Great effort in any endeavor always pays off.

10

Go To The Head Of The Stream

I<small>T'S AT THE HEAD</small> of the stream where the freshest water flows. It's at the head of a company where people making the business decisions have the ability to say, "yes". With every prospective business client, you will need to determine the answer to this question, "what is the decision-making process with this sales opportunity?" Find out if it is a decision by one or by committee? Who is that one person that can say, "yes", or who is the one person that can move it to the decision-making committee?

Finding the decision maker maybe the most critical piece of information to uncover early in the sales process. Who is THE person in a small business or a large corporation or in the "C" suite of a company that can say, "yes"? Much of your strategy going forward will be focused around finding that person. Hopefully it will take only one visit to find this answer.

Next, follow your discovery with the question, "What do you suggest is the best way to meet this person?" Or maybe, "Can you please assist me and introduce me to this person?"

There are lots of people in the sales process that can tell you "no". Most salespeople get bogged down visiting one person at a time in a company trying to work their way up the ladder to find the "yes". If you can determine the decision maker up front, you will save lots of time and many months, if not years, in the sales cycle.

Early in my twenties, I learned the importance of this principle when I was playing in Spring Training with the Los Angeles Dodgers. My "Granny" was a praying grandmother who liked to call me and find out how I was doing on a regular basis. During Spring Training, it gets rather hectic and the pressure of making a club is overwhelming. Calling "Granny" during Spring Training and sharing my day with her didn't happen consistently enough to her satisfaction.

One game day, I was riding the bus with my Dodger teammates to play the Houston Astros in Daytona Beach, Florida. I happened to be sitting with a Dodger great, first baseman, Steve Garvey, when Tommy Lasorda, our manager, entered the bus. Within minutes, Lasorda hollered out and asked, "Is Scotti Madison on the bus?"

Taken back, I answered, "yes sir" and immediately popped up and hurried to the front. Then Lasorda began his story, "Last night I was in bed with my wife Jo, and the phone rang,

'Hi, this is Scotti Madison's Granny … how's he doing?' So, I proceeded to talk with Granny for thirty minutes and she asked me all about my life. Then she began to ask about you. So, Madison, when you get home tonight … call your grandmother so, she won't call me again."

That evening I called Granny and asked her to please don't call my Manager, Tommy Lasorda, again. She said, "Well, I saw he was the head guy, and I knew he'd know how to get in touch with you." That's true, and I was afraid she might uncover the name Peter O'Malley, the team owner and she would call him next.

The quicker you find out who can say "yes", the sooner you make something good happen. Find out who lives at the head of the stream and begin to call on that person. It will save you a lot of time.

11

Everyone Deserves The Proper Respect

EVERYONE YOU MEET deserves to be greeted with a smile and kindness. It's critical that you are always polite and courteous and above all, show others honor and respect. Remember to show them reverence even when they act like a horse's rear end during your sales call. Respect is also relevant when it comes to a regard for authority. You must yield to a position of authority unless their actions are criminal or immoral. We find insight on both honor and respect in quotes like, "Let every soul be subject to governing authorities"; "Honor your father and mother".

Maybe start off by addressing your contact with a degree of respect by using either "Sir" or "Ma'am" during conversation. After you discover their name, I suggest you call everyone "Mr." or "Mrs.", followed by their last name until you are told differently. Even if they ask you to call them by their first name, you still might continue with "yes sir" and "no sir", "yes ma'am" and "no ma'am" … it's just good policy. Yes, I know it's old school, but demonstrating degrees of reverence to others bodes well on your character.

My defining moment on "honor and respect" occurred when I was twelve years old. It feels like yesterday, when I was at ball practice acting like a hyperactive "overly confident" little league shortstop. I was self-admiring that summer day as I was most days back then and acting quite "cocky" in front of my teammates. Then, I happened to notice my Dad parking his car in the left field lot just beyond the fence. Dad always found time to watch me practice. I saw him close his door and soon began strolling down the left field foul line headed towards third base. For some reason I had this urge to showily call out his name … not "Dad", not "Sir", but by his first name. What could possibly prompt such a death wish for a young boy? A demon must have possessed my body momentarily, certainly my tongue, when I hollered out, "Hey Charlie."

Time immediately stopped and the earth quit rotating for a moment. Crows began to fly overhead. It was as if an eclipse had occurred. All my teammates looked at me; some cried knowing they would never see me again. My Dad disgustingly stopped right where he stood, he never moved his body. His head spun to track my whereabouts with laser eyes wherever I went on the field. What was I thinking? I surely had lost my mind momentarily. The last time I saw that look on my Dad's face, he was about to kill a Buck Deer in the Alabama River swamps. I saw in my Dad's eyes a whipping was a ride home away.

Sensing how precious life was at this moment, I ran every ball down in the field and chased every foul ball hit. I carried all the equipment to the coach's car. Coach touched my shoulder and whispered, "I hope I see you again." As I approached my father, he never said a word. His head made a complete turn and rotated around his body, kind of like Linda Blair in the Exorcist. I knew this might possibly be my last car ride at the tender age of twelve.

When Dad entered the car and turned the key, I stared through the windshield as he spoke, "Son, let me make this perfectly clear. You will never, ever call me by my first name again. You will never call any adult by their first name. You will say, "yes sir" and "no sir", you will show respect to grownups from now on and I'm going to see to it when we get home." And he did.

That night my life was spared … I think maybe my father couldn't figure out how to dispose of my body. I had disrespected my Dad in front of everyone on the baseball field that day. I did not give him the honor he deserved being my father. And to this day, I still call everyone Mr. and Mrs. and say, "yes sir" and "yes ma'am", until I'm told differently. I learned a lot from that spanking. I learned to forget my Dad's first name. I learned people deserve your respect and you are to honor others in positions of authority all the time.

12

Be On Time ... All The Time

IF THERE IS ONE bad habit that drives me crazy, it is people being late to anything. I understand that things happen unexpectedly, but excuses like "bad traffic" or "the draw bridge caught me" are just not acceptable. Traffic has been around for some time and so has the dang bridge, so plan for it.

Vince Lombardi, the great Green Bay Packer coach, stated, "If you are five minutes early, you are already ten minutes late." I'm not suggesting being fifteen minutes early to everything, but you get the picture. Take notice that every person you call on who has ever played at a competitive level of sports in their life, you will discover they're always on time. In fact, usually they're early.

Case in point ... later in my life, I resurrected a friendship with my college baseball coach at Vanderbilt, Larry Schmittou. Coach Schmittou was quite the accomplished coach at Vanderbilt and was later a Professional Baseball Executive and currently a Bowling Magnate. His reputation is better than

P.T. Barnum at filling the seats in baseball stadiums. After he coached at Vanderbilt, he founded the Nashville Sounds; owned several other minor league teams; became an executive of the Texas Rangers and now owns Strike and Spare Lanes across three states. It doesn't matter what time he schedules to meet you; he is always ten minutes early. So, guess what ... he doesn't expect you to show up on time to meet him. His expectations whether consciously or unconsciously are for you to be there ten minutes early, just like him.

The point is being late anytime is simply unacceptable. It was unacceptable in the late 60's on Vince Lombardi's team and it's unacceptable today.

Remember, in sales you're always on someone else's time. It's the scarcest most finite resource of anything they have. When you're late or even the last to arrive at a scheduled event, you are perceived (fairly or unfairly) as being one of the following:

- **Inconsiderate**—You recognize you are late, and you just don't realize this shows little value for everyone else's time.

- **Rude**—You know you're late and you just don't care about anyone else's time.

- **Irresponsible**—You just didn't realize you were late. In fact, you never realize you're late, which is all the time, and you have no concept how your tardiness wastes other people's time.

- **Self-Important**—You know you're late but it's Ok. After all, what you were working on that caused you to be late was vastly more important than everyone else's trivial affairs they gave up being on time.

- **Disorganized**—You had the best of intentions to be on time, but the day just got away from you (as usual) and unfortunately you were late (again).
- **Self-absorbed**—You are just a jerk and don't care about anyone else or their time.

Most of the time ... inconsiderate, rude, flighty, self-important, disorganized jerks, don't make a sale. So, make the effort to be on time!

13

Trust The Person Who Fishes With Straws

You may be familiar with the name Vince Dooley. He was the legendary Head Coach of the Georgia Bulldogs for 25 years and won six Southeastern Conference championships. In 1980 he was selected the NCAA "Coach of the Year" after winning the national championship in football. The great running back Herschel Walker, whom I greatly admire, as well as Buck Belue, played on that team.

Every time I see Coach Dooley, Coach asks me to tell the story of the time he and my Dad went fishing off Perdido Key, Florida. Once Coach asked me to tell this story in front of 200 guests in Marietta, Georgia. I told his story at that luncheon just like he would tell it and Coach laughed along with the other attendees.

Coach Dooley first met my Dad when they played against each other in Alabama High School Football; Coach played at

McGill in Mobile and Dad played at Atmore. They later played against each other in College; my Dad played at Georgia and Coach Dooley played at Auburn. Coach always said that Charlie Madison was the toughest man he ever saw play football.

As the story goes just like Coach Dooley would tell it, "I'd been fishing at Gulf Shores with Fob James, the Governor of Alabama. We knew each other from Auburn. Fob had the biggest boat I'd been on, and we had fishing lines going out everywhere in the water. We didn't catch a fish that day. Didn't even get a bite. Barbara (Coach's wife) and I were headed back to Georgia when I told her, 'Charlie Madison lives over on Perdido Bay and for the past twenty years he's asked me to stop by and visit he and Sandra. We need to go over there before we head home, or he is going to wear me out asking to visit again.' So, we stopped over in Lillian and the first thing Charlie wants to do is go fishing. 'Charlie, I just went fishing yesterday with Fob James and we didn't catch a thing … I think it's a waste of time for us to go, they are just not biting', as we climbed into Charlie's 24-foot boat, half the size of Fob's."

"It was about a twenty-minute boat ride to the mouth of the Gulf when we headed into Perdido pass, which connects Perdido Bay with the Gulf of Mexico. It is right near the Florida – Alabama state line. Charlie stood up in the boat and motioned for me to take the wheel, 'Vince, steer the boat through the pass … I'm going to fix the bait.' I looked back at Charlie, and I swear… he was cutting up McDonald straws to use as bait. Back then the straws had red and gold swirls on them and evidently this was a new fishing secret for both King and Spanish Mackerel."

"'Charlie, what are you doing?'"

"'Vince, I'm fixing our bait to catch Spanish Mackerel'", as he sat in the back of the small boat and placed the cut McDonald straws around the hooks."

"I was a little concerned and thinking surely Charlie isn't serious, 'Look Charlie, I'm not sure what their paying you in insurance, but Georgia is paying me a good salary to be the head coach. I've got some money on me, so let's go over to the marina and I'll buy us some real bait.'"

"Charlie stood up and I could hear in his voice he was irritated. He pointed his finger at me and said, 'Vince, I know what I'm doing. Drive the dang boat … these straws are plenty good to fish with.'"

"I was a little scared of Charlie because I knew in his early years, he liked to fight, and he had fought everyone on the team at Georgia when he played. I thought if I said much more about the bait Charlie might throw me out of the boat. I just needed to trust that Charlie knew what he was doing and trust I wouldn't get tossed in water. So, I turned around, faced the Gulf of Mexico, and drove through Perdido Pass thinking this is another wasted day of fishing."

"To my surprise, we caught more Spanish Mackerel that day on those silly McDonald straws than you could've possibly imagined. It was the best day of fishing I've ever had. I'm glad I trusted Charlie and I'm so glad he didn't throw me out of the boat."

Sometimes you need to trust the person "who fishes with straws", training you on the company products and services even when it doesn't feel like they know what they're doing. After all, they have more experience "fishing with McDonald straws" than you do. Give your teachers and mentors the benefit of doubt; provide them with your undivided attention and do exactly as they say. If they are "catching fish", even in what seems to be an odd way, trust that their knowledge and personal experience in your field of sales will jump start your career.

14

"It's In Your Hands Now"

ONE SUMMER when I was playing with the Kansas City Royals, I strolled over to George Brett's locker. George may have been my all-time favorite player as a teammate. He played 21 seasons, won three batting titles and was a 13 x All-Star. He was not only a hall of fame player; he was completely dedicated to the game and possessed an exceptional work ethic. Every major league ball player respected George Brett's talent. Most of all, he was likeable, cordial and an outstanding teammate.

As I was chatting with him, I picked up one of his bats and began to swing it in the locker-room. The thought running through my head was, *'hey what if I used George's bat tonight; I bet I would get some hits? After all this guy is the only player in major league baseball who has won batting titles in three different decades. There must be some magic in his bat'.*

"Hey George, do you mind if I swing one of your bats tonight in the game?"

"No man, have at it. Grab one anytime", as George continued reading his fan mail.

"Hey thanks, you think this bat has any hits in it?" George looked at me, "Well, I don't know. Probably, but it's in your hands now."

I laughed and realized the magic wasn't in George Brett's bat, it was totally up to me. George was telling me that as good as George Brett is swinging a baseball bat, ultimately it was George Brett that determined the success. It was Scotti Madison that had the final say as to how well those bats would perform. I would be in control of my success or failure.

The same is true in any sales role in any company. Even when you are well prepared, as much as they've taught you, the only thing that matters is what you do with it. You ultimately are the one that must perform. The presentation and the results will eventually be determined "in your hands" and there is no one else that can go to the plate and hit for you. There will be a time when you must swing the bat, so go out and swing hard just in case you hit it.

15

"What We've Got Here Is A Failure To Communicate"

ONE OF MY all-time favorite movies was "Cool Hand Luke", starring Paul Newman. Newman was Luke Jackson, a prisoner in a Florida prison camp who refuses to submit to the system. When Luke, once again is being punished for not complying, he is standing before the warden (Strother Martin) when Luke is told, "What we've got here is a failure to communicate". It is truly one of the all-time quotes in a movie and is one of the most important sales lessons to learn.

Proper communication is everything and you must be able to find a way to both relate to your prospects and clients and effectively communicate your value proposition in a couple of minutes. At Vanderbilt, my professor Bobby Brooks would repeatedly state in his Business Policies and Management course, "Class, I don't care who your daddy is or who your mommy is, or how much your family trust is worth when you get out of Vanderbilt, if you can't relate to people, you are not going to make it in this world."

The best way to relate to others is to learn to effectively present your product then take a genuine interest in what they do and who they are and then listen carefully to their needs. You will never have a failure to communicate if you practice these principles.

16

It Can Always Be Worse ...
You Could Be In The Lunch Box League

REGARDLESS OF YOUR SITUATION, no matter how badly you feel, no matter how hopeless it appears, it can always be worse. Often, that's hard to imagine when life seems dreadful. But there will be the seasons of your life when hope feels like nothing more than a four-letter word. It's now when you need to stop the self-pity and take an outward sincere look at the lives of others. You will soon find someone near you whose circumstances are far worse.

Everyone has a story and when you take the time to listen to his or her story, you often find your problems really aren't that big. When you're dealing with a rebellious child, look around and you'll find someone who has lost his or her child. When you're suffering financial hardships, take a trip to the local mission and serve the homeless. When you're bedridden with back problems, you don't have to look far to find a veteran in a wheelchair with no legs. There's always someone out there who would love to have your problems and your worst days. I'm not negating your problem. I'm just trying to put your life in perspective.

Let me try and illustrate this in a story. After the first couple of seasons in the minor leagues, the better prospects would be invited to the Florida Instructional League, which was another two months of additional baseball training that took place in the fall season of the year. It would involve morning practices and then a nine-inning game starting around 1:00PM. One morning while traveling to Dunedin to play the Blue Jays team, we happened upon some construction traffic. It was a day on the bus when everyone felt tired; we were living in the grind of baseball after thirty-five straight days of practice. It had become a job for all of us and no longer our passion.

The bus was deathly quiet, when Jim Shellenback (Shelly), our pitching coach, began his disquisition on how it can always be worse, "Hey guys", arousing the entire bus, "See those guys out there, working in the hot sun, wearing orange and yellow hard hats?"

We all peered out the window at the highway construction crew. "Well, those guys would give anything to be riding this bus right now, practicing baseball every day and chasing a dream of playing in the major leagues. Everyone on this bus might be in the minor leagues right now, but those guys, those guys out there ... well, those guys are in the lunch box league.

You don't want to be in the lunch box league, because that's the league where you quit dreaming."

Wow! How profound! The "lunch box" league became our mantra for a time when you were ready to quit playing professional baseball and head home to an ordinary life. Shelly's observation reminded us to be grateful right where we are in life, to work through the grind, to appreciate the opportunity to work towards a dream and yes … it can always be worse.

Roman Emperor Marcus Aurelius wrote the book "Meditations", one of the more interesting secular books to read on self-improvement and building mental toughness. It involves a series of personal writings on self-improvement and in particular, Stoic Philosophy. It promotes a mind over matter lifestyle and one in which your feelings are completely discarded. In fact, it's Marcus's prescriptions to life written to himself for self-improvement. And besides all of that, his resiliency after losing nine children earns my respect. Personally, I wouldn't replace Christianity with Stoicism, but there are some profound ideas presented by the emperor.

- "When you arise in the morning, think what a privilege it is to be alive, to think, to enjoy, to love."
- "You have power over your mind … not outside events. Realize this and you will find strength."
- "It can only ruin your life if it ruins your character. Otherwise, it cannot harm you inside or out."

- "Today I escaped from my anxiety. Or no, I discarded it, because it was within me, in my own perceptions, not outside."

Marcus Aurelius advocated training your mind to be tougher than your situation and choosing a way out of your emotions. When you find your way to the "pity party", remember it can always be worse. Train your mind to stay out of the lunch box league and keep dreaming.

17

"Shoots For The Stars"

WILLIE MAE WAS MY grandparent's housekeeper and cook for some fifty years. When you work that long for a family, you're closer than blood relatives. My Mom always said, "Willie Mae helped raise me and she's better than family."

One time I was sitting in the kitchen in Benoit, Mississippi, during the Thanksgiving Holidays, feeling high anxiety. My uneasiness was due to me being slated as the starting quarterback for Vanderbilt in the upcoming game between Vanderbilt and the University of Tennessee. It was one week away, and UT was our biggest rival. It was a rivalry that was quite one-sided favoring UT over the years. After three years of hard work and relentless scout team duty, I was to be the starting Quarterback in our biggest game.

This November morning, I sat at the kitchen table replaying our offensive strategy over and over in my mind. I'm sure that Willie Mae noticed the distant look on my face, even while she was preparing our Thanksgiving Day meal. Willie Mae in her

60's, could have played the role of Aunt Jemima in 1893 for Quaker Oats Pancake mix. She stood beside me as she stirred a large bowl of dressing, "Youngen, what is going on with you? You look like you are far away from the Mississippi Delta."

Looking her way, "Yea Willie Mae, I'm a little nervous right now. See, I'm starting next week at Quarterback against Tennessee. It's the biggest game of my life and I'm a little nervous." I was feeling apprehensive worrying about the "what if's" in a football game with endless possibilities.

It was at this point in our memorable conversation that Willie Mae placed the mixing bowl full of cornbread, butter, celery, and onions, on the table. She pulled her chair out from the table, pushed her apron aside, sat down, leaned over a small kitchen table which is when her heart spoke to me, "You gots to have that confidence and aims high in life. Honeys child, shoots for the stars, cause if you land short, you still be on top of that mountain."

That was the last time I ever spoke with Willie Mae. I went back to Nashville a couple of days later and she passed away before I returned to the Delta that summer. She left me with some life changing words; profound thoughts swirling around in a Mississippi Delta kitchen. Willie Mae told me to set my goals high in life and if I'm a little short, it's all good, because I'm still an over achiever landing on top of the mountain. And being on top of the mountain … ain't all bad!

Some people don't like setting goals and cringe when they

hear the word "goal". They believe with goals comes undue self-pressure, and that can be true. Others don't set goals the right way. Just face it … goals do work. If you can set goals correctly, it enhances your personal expectations and good goals help dictate future performance. There is a big difference in telling someone to "do your best" compared to charting a course of success for them. People with goals usually succeed because they know where they're going. They don't allow pitfalls and tough times re-direct their journey nor end their pursuit of a worthy ideal.

I think there are far too many people in sales that don't set goals and when they do set them, they don't set their goals high enough. Aim high, higher than you think you can achieve and then work your tail off to reach your dreams. If you earnestly give it your best and remove undue self-pressure when goals are not achieved, recognize that you are not failing. Failing is not trying. Failing is not setting a goal. Earnestly working for a worthy goal is winning in sports, in sales and in life!

18

Success Doesn't Come In Torrential Downpours ... It Comes One Drop At A Time

There is nothing wrong with believing that you're going to close the biggest account your company has ever landed. If you're not a dreamer, then those long dry spells in the sales world will eat you up and you'll soon be packing up for another profession. To some degree, I think it's healthy and everyone should "shoots for the stars" in your heart and mind, as well as in your daily effort. But you also need to be realistic and recognize that sales success is more of a process than a one-time "get rich quick" phenomena.

There are so many success stories regarding men and women who worked hard to improve their "walk and talk" and have greatness thrust upon them. One of my favorite stories starting with humble beginnings, involves two very close friends I met on the beach at Pawley's Island, SC in the early 2000's.

Brian and Sassy Henry left Atlanta in 2002 and bought

and managed the historic Sea View Inn, a bed and breakfast place on Pawley's Island, SC. They were tired of the hustle and bustle and set out to raise their two young daughters in a more laid-back environment, the island community affectionately known as "arrogantly shabby". The 85-year-old inn, situated next door to me, soon became a huge success for the Henry's as they took such personal interest in all their guests that it became the "go to" place on the island for those who desired a charming step back in time experience with three excellent southern prepared meals a day. But that's not the success I'm talking about. What I'm referring to is their multi-million-dollar pimento cheese empire they built from Sassy's homemade recipe.

So how do you build a successful business selling plastic tubs of pimento cheese "one drop at time"? It starts by serving your pimento cheese recipe at the Atlanta Braves Playoff games in the 1990's and it's the hit of the tailgate parties. Next, you serve it to your bed and breakfast inn patrons on the shores of South Carolina and all the guests, buy it and take it home to share with other family and friends. Then around 2006 you take twelve small plastic containers of Sassy's pimento cheese to the Independent Seafood store in Georgetown, SC. They quickly sell out and Brian soon begins to use his applied background in marketing and sales calling on potential retailers. They later branch out to Food Lion, Piggly Wiggly and Publix and the rest is history. The pimento cheese now known as

"Palmetto Cheese" is known as the "The Pimento Cheese with Soul." Yet, if you really know Brian and Sassy, it's the pimento cheese created with love and compassion for other people, "one person at a time".

They took a recipe concocted in a family kitchen and turned it into the #1 cheese spread in America (Nielson 2019) now sold in over 9100 locations nationwide. So, when you're knocking on doors and wondering if you will ever make a sale, remember it took the Henry's 10 years from creation to sell their first tub of pimento cheese in a store and 14 years after that to become the most popular cheese spread in history. Success does not come in torrential downpours ... it comes one drop at a time.

19

Success Is Setting One Goal After Another

In 1980 WE WON the SEC championship in baseball at Vanderbilt, the very first one. This was quite an accomplishment for our team, and it was the one team goal we set before the season started. The problem was ... it was the ONLY team goal we set, and we accomplished it. We failed to even consider our next team goal, because we were so engrossed with goal number one. We should have looked ahead to additional goals to keep winning and eventually make it to the College World Series. We didn't aim high enough.

We lost out in the Regional Tournament in back-to-back games to the University of New Orleans and Florida State University. As I look back, we had the best team in the tournament, but we didn't expect to win because we had not set any additional goals past the SEC championship. Great teams continue to set goals after each victory until there are no more games left to play in the season.

Alexander Graham Bell once stated, "The achievement of one goal should be the starting point for another." Your goal is to set one goal after another on your journey of success. Achieving weekly goals will lead to monthly success and each month's victory will lead to annual success. Set small goals and once you hit your goal, immediately set another goal, then work hard to accomplish the next milestone. I believe depression comes upon us when we don't have anything to look forward to in life. That includes future goals.

20

Work For A Cause Greater Than Yourself

IT IS IMPORTANT to set personal goals to hit your sales numbers. As equally important, it's essential to find a greater cause than yourself to enhance your "walk and talk". Complete satisfaction in achieving a worthy ideal will never be found in individual achievements and will always involve either a team goal or providing a product or service that is instrumental to your customers well-being.

My uncle, Carl Madison, is one of the most successful coaches in high school history. He spent over 45 years coaching in numerous schools in Georgia, Florida and Alabama compiling a 326-129-7 record. Coach Madison is tied for second all-time in football victories in Florida. He was tough and practice was so hard that each day on the gridiron was a living hell. It was a matter of survival for all of us who dared to face up to his daily challenge. Practice was driven by physical toughness; repetition occurred until you mastered each play dozens of times in a row; there were no water breaks; the goal at every practice was to reach perfection and endure the hell until the Friday night lights glistened off your helmet.

Every day on the practice field at Tate High School in Northwest Florida, I could look to my left or right and see teammates lined up dedicated to winning. The pain I persisted through was no different than what my friends experienced. I saw my teammates survive a grueling practice and each player sacrificed academics, families, and social life ... all for the good of the team. There wasn't anything we wouldn't do for each other. We did whatever it took to taste the intoxicating nectar of victory. We ached all over when we lost a game. There was no one player more important than the good of the team. I cast my individual goals to tomorrow, and my only focus was on not letting my teammates down with the goal to win. Coming along beside each player for the benefit of a higher cause brought so much self-gratification that whatever I accomplished in individual recognition was a by-product of the greater good ... our team success.

What if you deliver a product or service that is so valuable, that you visibly watch your customers experience complete satisfaction from your deliverable? This is another way to set aside your personal goals for the good of the customer and the good of the team. Anything you sell should deliver a degree of fulfillment for your customer. Some products you sell may have a greater value than another, such as a heart valve compared to a bagel. The point is if you can deliver complete satisfaction to your customer and that's where you place your intrinsic worth, personal success is achieved. In doing so, you will experience a feeling of accomplishment far greater than the attainment of a personal sales goal.

In your career, find that cause greater than yourself. It will make your business sales career far more enjoyable.

21

Passion Is The Game

ONE WAY TO sell out of inspiration is to walk with passion in whatever you're doing. Passion doesn't come from your company's expertise in your industry or your superior product. Real passion that lasts comes from within the depths of one's soul. It comes from an internal drive that is fueled by quiet time; self-reflection; reading something encouraging; or reading about someone who overcame incredible odds. It comes from deep inside one's desire to do something great and requires a deep love for what you're doing. You cannot enjoy your sales position unless you have passion for your role.

It's not easy to have passion everyday, because life's pressures can be very real and after all … you are human. To overcome reality, you must often change your mindset. You should be tougher than your situation and it comes from training your mind every day to think positive and to carry onward even when it feels impossible. Passion will help you fight through the circumstances that attempt to beat you down.

I played with numerous players in baseball that loved the game, but the one player I have in mind when it comes to passion was Greg "Smooch" Smith. I don't know how Greg got the nickname "Smooch" and let's be clear, this is the African American Greg Smith. You know "smooch" means to kiss and cuddle amorously. I can say with complete confidence if Greg Smith could've found a way to marry a baseball, he would've done it. He loved playing the game of baseball more than anyone I've ever met.

I first remember Greg when I played against him in the California League when he played for the Lodi Dodgers. He played first and when an opposing player reached first base, Greg with a huge smile on his face, would just chat with you, "How you doing today, man? Boy isn't it a great day to play baseball? I wish we could play two."

Then I had the privilege to play with "Smooch" in Texas in 1982 for the San Antonio Dodgers. Often, he was the first person to show up to the ballpark, sometimes arriving ahead of those that worked on the grounds crew. He would arrive early and just play toss against some brick wall at the stadium while carrying on a conversation with some local kids. "Smooch" would afford a dumpy apartment near the ballpark then walk home after the game. He'd carry his uniform, wash it that night and then walk back to the park the next day sometimes wearing his uniform. On the road, I'd see him at times walking around on the streets in Little Rock, AR or El Paso, TX or Amarillo, TX proudly wearing his San Antonio Dodger uniform. He would stroll through town greeting people, extending kindness, and inviting everyone he met to the game that night.

He was the ambassador of baseball. His passion for baseball was at another level compared to my love for the game. "Smooch" absolutely loved the game, and I knew one day he'd want to be buried in his baseball uniform. I often wonder where he is today. His dedication is the kind of passion that takes your "walk and talk" to another level.

I think passion is overcoming the difficulties and maintaining the joy in the process. It's the strong feeling of enthusiasm or excitement for something or someone. Don't you just love being in the presence of someone who believes in their product, or a worthy ideal or something so incredible, that their excitement overflows from their heart? Their excitement comes in enjoying the process, not in completed sales. Passion demonstrates your complete commitment, and it takes great passion to become a great salesperson.

22

Inspirational Mentors Are The Only Shortcut

THERE ARE TRULY no shortcuts to success in life. You must pay your dues; do the work and put in your time. If there is a shortcut, it might be finding others who have been in sales longer than you that can possibly deliver insight thereby reducing some future mistakes. And I say "reduce", not "eliminate", because you will still make mistakes.

Sales have been around since the very first business. Nothing ever happens in business until "a sale is made". So, there are other people in your line of work, more successful, older, more experienced who have blazed a trail in sales long before you considered the profession. Seek and find those people! Learn from their success and mistakes; learn through their sale's life experiences and from their personal trials and tribulations. If you are just getting started in sales, find a mentor!

I remember a special moment in Chicago when I spent a day with my mentors. I was with the Detroit Tigers, and we were playing a three-game series against the White Sox. I was sitting in the hotel lobby, dressed in a coat and tie, which was the required dress code of a professional ball player under Tiger manager Sparky Anderson. I was new to the Big Leagues and new to the Tigers, and I was anxious to rub elbows with some of the veterans. It wasn't long before Lance Parrish our catcher and two great pitchers, Jack Morris, and Dan Petry, walked off the elevator. They saw me in the hotel lobby and asked me to join them for a stroll down Michigan Avenue. That day I listened to their stories … occasionally questioning their daily approach to the game. They were veterans who were stars on the 1984 World Series Champion Tigers a year earlier.

Well, I learned a lot that day walking in Chicago. I learned I would be carrying all the apparel items they purchased in the stores up and down Michigan avenue. I carried boxes of shoes, bags of shirts and pants for all three. I was loaded down like a pack mule. They did buy me a nice pair of shoes for carrying all their items. Yea, they needed someone to carry their shopping bags, but in turn, I spent a quality day hanging with some great veteran-mentors learning the ins and outs of a Major League Baseball player.

Seek and learn what's essential from those who are the best and have cut the trail before you. Find someone who preceded you in failures and successes. It could be a valuable shortcut that saves you years of unnecessary trials and tribulations. It's the only allowed shortcut in your business career.

23

Embrace "Constructive Criticism"

Growing up as a child, my father was always giving me valid and well-reasoned advice in a "no nonsense" manner. He wasn't concerned how it made me feel. He was more concerned on how it improved me as a person. He just expected me to heed his advice and do better. When my Dad corrected me, he always referred to it as "constructive criticism". He would say something like this, "Son, I'm giving you some constructive criticism right now because I love you. I know you can do better than what you're doing. I want you to remember this … the day I quit getting on you, is the day I don't believe you can do any better. You don't want that day to ever happen. That'll be a sad day for you and me."

Maybe you just can't handle somebody correcting you; you don't take constructive criticism well… even when it comes from someone who really cares about your life. You need to allow yourself to be vulnerable and open to feed back when it makes you a better person. Learn to embrace constructive words gracefully which may be in the form of criticism, even those words that cut to the heart. If it's for your good, you must set your feelings aside and allow someone's constructive advice to make you a better person. The feedback is a blessing when you are learning about the obstacles you must overcome to maximize your potential.

Besides family members who should be honest with you, even your best friends need to criticize you when you are out of line. I have about four or five very close friends that are brutally honest with me. There was a time in my life when I wasn't acting right (actually several), and three of my friends called me in on the carpet. I joined them for lunch, and they told me my recent behavior was unacceptable and destructive. I knew they cared for me, so I shamefully apologized, "Guys thanks for letting me know. I won't do that again." I know it was my father's early interventions that prepared me to be able to accept constructive criticism from my friends.

You hope friends come along in your life that have the integrity and courage to correct you out of love. Then your role is to be big enough and humble enough to heed their advice. If you're looking to become the very best person, then welcome direct comments that cut to the quick. You never want there to come a day when those closest to you give up on you and quit giving you encouragement and direction affectionally known as "constructive criticism".

24

Don't Take Yourself So Seriously

Sometimes it's easy to take your position in life too seriously. You think you have a far more prominent role in making the world go around than you actually might. Maybe some early sales success went to your head and inflated your ego. I think to gain a healthy perspective on life, learn to laugh at yourself. No matter how serious your life requires you to be or how good you are at something; you better keep things in perspective and learn to expect your high accomplishments with humility, as well as brush off your failures.

My best lesson in life at learning to laugh at myself was a joke played at my expense by none other than the legendary coach Tommy Lasorda of the Los Angeles Dodgers. This happened in 1982 at Spring Training and my exuberance and hustle as a player set me up for the joke. I was the over hustling player in the Dodger camp and teammates such as Dusty

Baker, Steve Sax and Steve Garvey kept telling me, "Hey you are making us look bad. You are over hustling. Slow down!" It was obvious to every player and coach how hard I worked. I never saw any playing time, but that didn't discourage me. I certainly was a go-getter. My locker room was in the same building and adjacent to the Big-League players locker room. There were about twelve other players with me who were non-roster players in camp this particular Grapefruit League season and we were living the dream. After all, this was the Los Angeles Dodgers, the 1981 World Series Championship team and the presence of Hollywood happened every day in Dodgertown.

Mark Cresse, who coached with the Dodgers from 1974 to 1998, was as good a person as you could ever meet. Mark was Tommy Lasorda's full time bull pen coach and part time messenger boy, so Tommy sent Mark to retrieve me one morning. His words were direct and simple, "Tommy needs to see you now."

I was highly optimistic walking into Tommy's office. The Grapefruit League for the Big Leaguers was ending in about five days and the team was heading to Los Angeles to begin the regular season. I knew my hustle had not only given me a good name but had set me on a path to the big leagues. There is a term called "unrealistic expectations" and I was sitting front and center.

I walked into Tommy's office, and it was standing room

only with coaches, Joey Amalfitano, Danny Ozark, Ron Perranoski, Manny Mota; and making a guest appearance was Sandy Koufax. This was quite the list of baseball legends, and I was at a loss for words. Each began to tell me, "Good job Scotti! Way to hustle! You play the game hard!" Then Tommy began to take over the conversation, "Scotti Madison bleeds Dodger blue. No one plays like he does. If everyone came to the park every day and played as hard as he does the Dodgers would win the World Series every year." Lasorda then asked the group to leave his office stating, "I want to talk to Scotti alone."

As the entire room emptied, each coach was patting me on the back, "Keep up the good work." At this point in time, I believed without a shadow of a doubt that I had made the Dodger team. Why else would I receive such praise? I had never even swung a bat in a spring training game, yet what did that matter? I was about to make this team, or so I thought.

Lasorda continued to sing my praises for at least another five minutes or so, and then he said, "Hey I need you to step over here," which of course I did. Lasorda opened a side door to his office, which was the entrance into his personal bathroom. While he continued to talk about the Dodger blue in the sky and how much I hustled, without missing a beat, he dropped his baseball britches and sat right smack on the bathroom toilet.

This was a first for me and I was not quite sure just how to respond to this foolhardy display from Tommy. Visualize the most recognizable manager in professional baseball, sitting on the "john" singing your praises. Tommy was perched only 6-8 feet away and I was not sure what to do. I was just trying to find a fresh air pocket for some relief from this man who loved Italian food. Soon my eyes began to water, and I finally responded, "Hey Tommy I really appreciate the talk, but is it ok if we finish this conversation later?"

"Sure", Tommy said. Upon exiting out to the hall, I noticed all the coaches standing near the door. They were holding stopwatches in their hands and timing my perseverance. When I recognized I had been played, a huge laugh echoed among the coaches. I was informed that I may have set a record in Spring Training enduring Tommy Lasorda's favorite joke.

Tommy never spoke to me again. I played Double A baseball that season. It was the best joke ever played on me. It taught me not to take myself so seriously. Neither should you!

25

The Right Place At The Right Time Works Best When You Are Well Prepared

IN MALCOLM CALDWELL'S BOOK, "Outliers", he highlights the importance of preparation that determines the success of individuals. Although opportunity and timing, which one might refer to as "being at the right place at the right time" often are critical in the launch of exceptional results, every person who experienced success was extremely prepared at that moment in time when perfect timing appeared to launch his/her success.

One such person or group that Caldwell uses as his example were the Beatles. They are without a doubt the most successful band in the history of music. Anyone who has ever followed the Beatles would probably point to their beginning of fame to the night they performed on the Ed Sullivan show.

On February 9, 1964, me at six years old and a record setting 73 million other people tuned in to watch four guys in Edwardian suits and mop top haircuts. It left such an impressionable mark on me that I can remember sitting on a couch with my parents and my Dad complaining, "Why would anyone listen to foreigners with long hair play such strange music?"

Coming from a man sporting a crew cut, his continuous mantra was, "They all need haircuts". I don't think Dad ever saw the significance of this evening.

This happened to be the Beatles first week in the US and they appeared to be so comfortable performing live in the moment that they created one of the most seminal moments in television history. Their performance on the Ed Sullivan Show immediately launched Beatlemania to international fame.

What prepared John, Paul, George and Ringo to appear so comfortable at this critical stage in their life, under great pressure to perform live at the highest possible level to a television audience around the world? For starters, for a period of three years prior to the show, they practiced or performed an average of 6 - 8 hours per day for about 270 days and nights annually. By the time they arrived in the United States and were playing on stage for the Ed Sullivan show, they had performed live as a band over 1000 times making them adequately prepared when the opportunity to take the stage came knocking at their door. In fact, they were far better than adequately prepared.

I acknowledge the importance of timing or opportunity, or as some might refer to it as "blind luck". It certainly is an important component in the success of many an exceptional person. But, don't downplay the importance of being fully prepared when the timing to perform is right before you. The Beatles had achieved expert status due to the relentless practice they performed over and over mastering their profession. They probably never looked at the Ed Sullivan Show as a make-or-break performance for the band. It was just another time of performing out of some 1000 times they played during the prior three years. Be prepared when your lifetime chance arrives.

My favorite personal story of timing and preparation involves Coach Woodrow McCorvey, recently retired from Clemson University. (Google "Dabo Swinney shares moment with Woodrow McCorvey after winning Coach of the Year"- It is very moving) Woody, as his close friends call him has coached on numerous NCAA championship teams.

After coaching at Alabama A&M in 1979, Woody moved and coached at Clemson, Alabama, Tennessee, South Carolina, Mississippi State, and Clemson again. His coaching roles involved quarterbacks, wide receivers, tight ends, running backs and he served as the offensive coordinator. He was on National Championship teams at Clemson under Danny Ford; Alabama under Gene Stallings; Tennessee under Phillip Fulmer; Clemson under Dabo Swinny and won dozens of Conference Championships, as well. His timing being on the right team was exceptional and Coach would tell you he was blessed. But what the average person doesn't know is that

Coach McCorvey paid his dues and was well prepared for each opportunity. His first six years in coaching was at Tate High School in Pensacola, Florida. I know his days were long and difficult, because he coached for my uncle, Carl Madison. Woody was one of my coaches for three seasons. He was well prepared to be an impactful coach for young men long before he hit the college scene.

26

Practice Self-Discipline Even When It Hurts

If you plan on being exceptional in sales, if you plan on being an exceptional parent, if you plan on being an exceptional friend, if you want to be exceptional at anything, it's vital that you practice self-discipline in your life. I've never met anyone in life that is successful in any field or endeavor who is not self-motivated and leads a life of self-discipline.

What does it mean to be self-disciplined? It's the ability to wake up early without an alarm; it's always being on time for a meeting; it's making time during your day to better yourself through inspirational books and stories; it's waking up early to prepare your kid's breakfast before school; it's taking care of your personal health and hygiene; it's not allowing your weakness to take over your life. The actual definition involves "controlling one's feelings and overcoming one's weaknesses, as well as the ability to pursue what one thinks is right despite temptations to abandon it."

Life isn't easy when we chase a dream because the work required to obtain it may begin to feel like drudgery and your lifelong objective evolves into a menial task. When the pursuit of your dream feels like a full-time job or the pursuit of a greater cause feels like drudgery, the intrinsic satisfaction felt through disciplining your mind is no longer self-gratifying.

I remember a time while playing for the Kansas City Royals that I was in the bullpen at Royals Stadium. I was sitting beside Daniel Raymond Quisenberry, better known as Quiz. He was as an exceptional person as you could ever meet; a deep thinker; an amiable man full of laughter and good cheer.

This particular day in Royals Stadium sitting in the bullpen, Dan Quisenberry was not in a jovial mood. Quiz was not pitching well, and he'd lost his magic on the mound. From 1980 – 1985, Quiz had averaged 32.5 saves a season and had been rewarded with a lifetime contract that stretched into 2025. It involved real estate holdings and some other odd details but was worth around $50 million. Now it was June of 1988 and Quiz had three save opportunities in the past 11 months. What once was a profession filled with highlights and living his dream in major league baseball had become a tormentous job for Dan Quisenberry.

The look of anguish was on Quiz's face as he spoke, "Scotti, I'm as miserable as I've ever been in life. I'm not getting the job done on the mound. That's never happened to me before. I don't know what to do."

I felt for Dan because he was such a good guy. I mostly listened and provided little more than an ear for his troubles, because I couldn't relate to his baseball success or the money he was making. "Quiz, it'll come back. You'll be OK."

Quiz was flipping a baseball in his right hand with his thumb over and over, "You know anyone can play this game when you're going good. It takes a hell of a person to play it when you're going badly. And that's where I am now… going really bad. The only thing rewarding for me right now is to stay true to myself. I've got to tell my mind to keep on going even when I don't want to. Self-discipline hurts right now."

Quiz was right. It's important that we still exercise self-discipline and stay true to your self, especially when we're going badly. We will be rewarded for such self-dedication, but not always. Dan Quisenberry never made it back to his all-star form and two years later in 1990 he retired wearing a San Francisco Giants uniform. His self-discipline began many years earlier, probably as far back as high school, and his reward was his baseball success, his lifetime contract and his impeccable character that left a legacy for his family. Dan is dearly missed!

27

People Buy From Good People With Common Ground

BEING A GOOD PERSON is a critical quality action that does nothing but benefit you early on and can carry forward for a lifetime. When developing your "walk and talk" habits, it is crucial to be a friend to everyone. It's about making an effort to find something in common that allows you to connect with someone on a deeper level. With common ground comes common understanding and mutual appreciation for each other. When you can connect with someone finding similarities, it allows a friendship to grow. People would rather buy from others they see as a friend and always will. No matter how different and unique people are, there is bound to be some common ground between a seller and buyer if you are willing to make the effort to find it.

Start by looking for common interests, like experiences or similar beliefs and views. Of course, be tactful and thoughtful in your efforts to make friends. Be genuine in your approach and sincere in everything when it comes to learning the background about prospective clients. It may require some homework behind the scenes. Perhaps look at LinkedIn or even their Facebook page. Make calls to friends to see if anyone possibly knows your point of contact.

Upon entering their world (office or workplace), scan the walls and look at their photos and their memorabilia. Potential clients will tell a story about themselves through pictures and plaques. Their lives read like a book across the walls of their office space where they spend much of their life.

Most people will talk about their passions. If they are blessed with a family, their favorite subject matter is usually their children, good or bad. After the initial connection, are you willing to invest the time it truly takes to begin to care about someone else's life? Finding that common ground may lengthen the sales cycle, but the ability to genuinely relate to someone as a friend will pay dividends for a lifetime. But, don't expect an instant friendship just because you share common ground. What you have is a good start to building a lasting friendship. It takes time and effort, and you must be willing to nurture that relationship.

I once called on a company in Nashville, Tennessee, Rogers Group. I was visiting Gail Frye, the head of HR one day and she asked me a pointed question, "Scotti, how long have you been calling on us?"

"Well, Gail, I think it's been ten years."

Then she totally surprised me, "Really ten years? That long? By the way, what do you do for a living anyway?"

I may have gone a little overboard on nurturing that business relationship. If there was such a thing as focusing on common ground too much and becoming a friend, I had reached it. During those ten years, I quit trying to sell her a product and appreciated our common interests. I really enjoyed Gail's friendship and company. Heck, when my kids were born, I took them both over as babies to her offices in Metro Center. I saw Gail's daughter play softball several times over the years. Finally, after years of visits, Gail Frye and Roger's Group did business with me that year and were a loyal client for eight years until I left Nashville.

28

If You Talk To Someone About Their Money Or Their Honey, It's Best To Eyeball Them

WE HAVE ENTERED an era when many sales are made over the phone and even more sales are completed online. It's a time when personal contact and sales conversation might be a passing parade. Yet, I believe if you're going to talk with someone about any exchange of money taking place, which a sale usually comprises, do that in person as much as possible.

When spending money and making a business decision, would you rather meet with your salesperson or would you prefer a phone call? Now we have Skype, Zoom and face time, which is "like" live, but not really live. However, there is nothing like looking into a potential client's eyes when a decision must be made. Face to face is vital in making a lasting impression in a sale. Besides, it's harder for them to say "no" when you ask for their business in person.

I remember the last test I took at Vanderbilt University. It was a Business Finance class and Ted Day was my professor. I wasn't doing so well early on in class, probably because I was taking both an accounting and calculus class at the same time. I was drowning in my studies. Heading into my Business Finance final, I was looking at an average of 49. I stopped by numerous times during the semester and visited with Professor Day, making it clear I had to pass his finance class to graduate from Vanderbilt.

He informed me, "Well Scotti, I'm not quite sure what you'll make in this class. Right now, you're failing my course and it will take an exceptional score on the final to raise it up to a "D". The final is worth 35% of the class grade. I wish you the best. After the test next week, you can call my office and I'll share your result."

Well, if I was going to fail, Professor Day was going to have to fail me in person. I was not going to let him fail me over the phone. After taking my final exam in college, I showed up at his office expecting to beg him for my passing grade.

Professor Day began, "Scotti, I'm a little surprised at your test results." Anticipating a poor performance, I cringed and immediately began to plead for mercy, "Sir, please ... I really need to pass your class."

"Oh, passing my class is not the problem. I'm not sure what to give you. In fact, you made the highest grade on the final by some ten points. It's obvious you understand the material better than anyone in my class, so I've decided to give you an 'A'."

Whoa…that's graduating with a bang! To this day I know personally visiting Professor Day numerous times paid off. So, if you have time to make the one-on-one acquaintance of your buyer or professor, make the personal connection and make it often. You could end up with an "A" grade when everything else points to a "D".

29

"Let Me Think About It?"

I FIND THE MOST DIFFICULT reply in sales to overcome is "let me think about it". That's not really a "yes" and it's not even a "no". Basically, they're saying, "I have other things that are a priority right now and I just don't feel like making a decision".

It's certainly better than a direct "no, we're not interested". Yet, this dichotomy of sorts sets up your next approach, which is to move this particular response back into the "opportunity" column?

It's important that you find out if this is just a nice way to get rid of you or truly, they're just not ready to decide because he/she has not received enough information to make an informed confident decision. How do you move the sale further down the line without offending the prospect?

Consider asking nicely, "How long would you like to think about this and is there anything else we can provide to help you with your decision?" You will probably receive a response and move the needle off stalemate. I think my most powerful and bold response can be used if you have spent numerous times pursuing this prospect, "I appreciate your frankness, can you help me understand as to why you would not want to do business with us?" This pointed question is bold, but you will get an answer.

Once I was sitting in a meeting with HMA, Health Management Associates out of Naples, Florida. We were one of three presentations that day to their executive committee, which included my friend Wayne Neiswender, and were last to present. During the meeting, I just sensed it in their body language that they were tired, had lost interest in the process and a decision would not be made. They were slumping down in their chair, looking at their watches, doodling on paper, and nodding off, which said more to me than words.

It was time to sink or swim which is when I asked, "I wonder if we can skip the power point today and just have some conversation at the conference table?" Letting out a big sigh, they all said, "That would be great."

Rather than my standard question "why would you not want to do business with us", I tried a different approach. This day in Naples I tried the opposite approach, "You invited us in to make a presentation on our voluntary benefits at Aflac. I was wondering if you could tell me why you would even consider doing business with us? What do you like about our company?"

I stayed quiet and Ray Melvin, my partner in this business opportunity, gasped for air when he heard me ask that piercing question. We waited and waited at what seemed like an eternity before they responded. Finally, they proceeded to tell us everything they liked about Aflac and in fifteen minutes they had convinced themselves that we were the best company to insure their 20,000 employees. We never made a presentation. HMA would be one of Aflac's top five clients for many years.

30

Train Your Mind To Think Winning Thoughts

ONE OF THE BEST BOOKS on understanding the importance of attitude is "Man's Search for Meaning" by Victor Frankl. Frankl wrote about his confinement in a Nazi Prisoner of war camp. After reading his book and then personally visiting Yad Vashem, the Israeli Holocaust Museum in Jerusalem, it completed a picture in my mind of the atrocities that Frankl experienced. The torture and pain he lived through must have been unbearable. Shockingly the German soldiers documented these acts of barbarity, so they could educate future generations on how to destroy an entire race. It is in this light that Frankl coined what I consider to be the most powerful secular phrase ever constructed about attitude:

"Everything can be taken from a man, but one thing, the last of the human freedoms – to choose one's attitude in any given set of circumstances, to choose one's own way."

How powerful are those words? You can successfully train your mind to respond to any adversity, any disappointment, or any unsuccessful sales call. So, when someone says "no", when someone is rude to you, when someone tries to steal your dream, you have the power to control how you respond to a negative situation. You ultimately have the power to overcome any adversity.

Between stimulus and response there is this space that exists in the mind. Within that space is the power to choose your response. Your response governs how you grow as a person and how you build up your "walk and talk" in life. This is the place where God has created in you your "choice" mechanism. In that power of response your entire freedom as a human being resides. How you choose to answer any given hardship will determine your character journey.

In sales, it's your attitude that empowers you to get past a "no" and continue on in life until you hear the word "yes." Someone who is striving to improve your "everything else" that you possess will train himself or herself to reply to a "no" in a positive manner. When you can train your mind to accept the good and the bad in a positive manner, you have conquered maybe the hardest part of both sales and life.

31

There Is No Such Thing As A Stupid Question

To FIND OUT someone's needs and objections, you prompt them hoping to begin a dialog of questions. When a prospect asks questions, they show interest in your product or service. Good questions are considered a buying sign and buying signs are always welcome. Try to follow up their question with a question of your own. Prospects who ask questions are usually more willing to answer the questions you have of them. That's the best way to learn about your customer.

It's important to note that any question they ask you should be treated as a good question. Every time someone asks you a question, extend to him or her a positive affirmation, "That's a good question." This demonstrates diplomacy on your part and encourages more questions from the prospect. When they ask questions, it opens the door for you to ask more questions of them. This type of dialog develops the "trust factor" and delivers better sales results.

The Late Coach Mal Moore, the former Athletic Director at the University of Alabama and longtime defensive assistant coach under the great Paul "Bear" Bryant, once told us one of his favorite stories. Coach Moore coached with Bear Bryant for some twenty years. He also was responsible for bringing Coach Nick Saban to Alabama. I had the privilege of dining with the famed Coach Moore three times in a private setting with his close friends. It was in this environment he felt comfortable enough to share some stories that would be considered "inside stories".

One night at dinner at the University of Alabama's President, Bob Witt's campus home, Coach Moore began, "Every Monday the Birmingham quarterback club would host a lunch. Coach Bryant, the guest of honor, would speak about the previous Saturday football game. He was always humble, blaming himself for the loss or for the team not playing well in a thirty-point win. Coach would take up all of the time and then immediately head back to Tuscaloosa. It was always faithfully attended by close to five hundred loyal Bama fans. Coach never fielded questions, and nobody would dare ask one. Strangely one day, Coach Bryant ended his talk early and said, 'I think I might take some questions today from some of ya'll.' Well, every person in the entire room raised their hands hoping Coach Bryant would call on them. Coach saw the large response, paused, then leaned into the microphone, 'Let me make something perfectly clear, I don't want any stupid questions.' Immediately everyone dropped their hands and Coach Bryant walked out of the building. Coach never fielded a question that day nor any other time at the Birmingham Quarterback Club for twenty-five years."

32

Always Be Learning

THERE WAS A TIME soon after college that I called on Thompson and Green Caterpillar to solicit them for insurance. In particular, I met with Dewitt C. Thompson III. He attended Vanderbilt University before enlisting in the Army Air Corps, where he served as a flight instructor throughout World War II. He remained a faithful supporter of the Vanderbilt Football program, which is how I arranged the meeting.

I was a little nervous because Dewitt III and his brother, Hall Thompson of Birmingham and Shoal Creek, PGA, fame, owned the Caterpillar dealerships in Middle Tennessee and Birmingham. Dewitt III was the prototypical patriarch of a large and established Nashville family of stature. They were above my pedigree, yet all of them were always considerably kind to me.

I remember entering Mr. Thompson's office; the room

looked like a library with an insurmountable number of books behind a large oak desk. They were neatly stuffed in the shelves, but you could tell they were well read and served more than just a backdrop. I was offered a seat in one of the two chairs immediately in front of Mr. Thompson's throne.

He opened the conversation as I peered at the photos on the wall that defined the history of a life well lived and that of a seasoned businessman, "Son what can I do for you today?"

"Mr. Thompson, Sir, I'm with Aflac and do you know anything about supplemental insurance", fidgeting in my seat at what may have been my fourth presentation.

Then something happened in the conversation… somehow, I misused the word "rapport" in a sentence and Mr. Thompson leaned into the conversation, "What did you say? I don't think you used that word correctly."

"Uh … Sir, what word", as I began to rethink my conversation.

"The word you just said, 'rapport' … I think you misused it when you spoke", commenting while he stood up and reached for a dictionary high on his bookshelf.

I suddenly felt incredibly small when Mr. Thompson turned the pages to the "R's" in his big Webster's Dictionary, "Here it is right here … reading the page … 'rapport' … 'a close and harmonious relationship in which the people or groups concerned understand each other's feelings or ideas and communicate well.' Yes, you did misuse the word."

I sat peering at him across his desk of papers and Mr. Thompson seemed to be moving further and further away from me as the room grew bigger. I couldn't find a breath and my tongue was stuck to the roof of my mouth. I knew my presentation had come to an end. I about fainted when I stood up, "Thank you Sir for bringing that to my attention, I will remember that ...have a good day", and I walked out his door. I never saw Mr. Thompson again.

I went straight to a bookstore and bought a dictionary. From that day going forward, every letter I've ever written, every paragraph I've typed, I've had a dictionary right beside me. Now, I look up words constantly on my laptop. That was not only one of the most embarrassing moments of my life; it proved to be one of the more beneficial and a valuable lesson. Here I was a graduate of Vanderbilt University, carelessly thinking highly of myself and assuming my education was complete. After all, how much smarter could I be? That monumental day I learned my education in both life and business was just beginning. Never be satisfied with your level of knowledge, and always be learning.

It serves you soundly to be well spoken, well-educated and well versed in many topics. A growth mindset far outweighs one that is fixed. Never be satisfied in the knowledge attained today, for tomorrow something new will cross your path. After all, a continuous thirst for knowledge may allow you to have a better "rapport" with your clients.

33

Find Their Pain, Feel Their Pain, Stop Their Pain

DURING MY FIRST SUMMER in professional baseball, I was playing for the Orlando Twins, the Double A Farm Club of the Minnesota Twins. Our trainer was Wayne "Big Fella" Hattaway. You might want to Wikipedia him to get the entire picture of "Big Fella". Keeping it short, let's just say Wayne was a nice, happy-go-lucky fellow and very "unique".

"Big Fella" was from Mobile, Alabama; believed wrestling was real; wore Star Wars socks; loved Alabama Football and was the practicing Trainer/Equipment Manager on the Double A Twins. He had "0" medical knowledge or college education. This was the Twins and Mr. Calvin Griffith was all about saving money. The need for an appropriate medical background would only come into play if you provide medical assistance to professional athletes ... which oddly Wayne did every day.

One game in July, one of our players slid into second base resulting in a compound ankle fracture. When Wayne ran on to the field to care for the injured player, he wasn't expecting to see an open wound with a protruding bone. Wayne's job, like every good trainer, was to find the injured players pain and stop his pain ASAP. This time, it didn't happen that way. Wayne saw the bone protruding out from the sock and he passed out right there on the field near second base. "Big Fella" obviously found the pain and it got the best of him.

Regardless of the product you're pushing, if the prospect doesn't see a need for it, there will never be a sale. Uncovering where there is a need specific to your product or service is vital. Then your presentation can be lasered to solving their exact problem. If they don't have a problem, help them see a problem in which they were earlier unaware. Seeing your product or service as the solution to their pain, often results in a completed sale.

To illustrate the point, when I was selling Cancer insurance for Aflac, everyone had good major medical insurance. They couldn't see how an illness like cancer could cause them to lose any money considering almost 100% of their medical expense was completely covered before Obama Care.

So, I had to make them aware of something they didn't know existed, non-medical costs. For example, when someone has cancer there will be possible travel to treatment centers, loss of income from one or both family members and every day expenses incurring additional costs. This was all true and anyone who's ever battled the dreadful illness has experienced the extra expense. Making them aware of a common problem in treating cancer became uncomfortable to them. They then saw the need for our policy that would give them cash to take care of a possible future financial pain.

I made them aware of a scenario that had a good probability of occurring since statistically they had a one in four chance of cancer striking their family. They recognized a perceived problem that I brought to their attention and then I helped them by providing a solution, which was a policy that paid out cash dollars.

Whatever you're pushing, if the prospect doesn't see a need or their pain doesn't make them feel uncomfortable, you will not make a sale.

34

Set Expectations Early

I'VE HAD THE PRIVILEGE over a six-year period to work with Dr. Dimitris Bertsimas who is maybe the brightest person I've ever known. He is the Boeing Leaders for Global Operations Professor of Management, the Co-Director of the Operations Research Center, and the Director of the Master of Business Analytics at MIT. That was a mouthful but like I said, he is a smart fellow.

It's rare that someone with "book smarts" communicates effectively in a sales/business setting, but that's not the case with Dr. Bertsimas. In every meeting I have jointly attended, Dr. Bertsimas and our CEO, Stephen Sofoul, a MIT graduate, would tag team the client and perform an outstanding job of setting expectations when the meeting begins. In other words, at the onset for each meeting, they brought forth the expectations for both sides, so it is obvious as to what simultaneous goals must be achieved. Their common question is, "Today when we walk away from our meeting, what would you like to see accomplished? What are your expectations today?"

I have repeatedly used this business strategy in every meeting since I first heard Dr. Bertsimas and Stephen make their case. Asking your prospective customer up front what they would like their "take away" to be allows you to quickly learn exactly what your prospect has in mind and where the conversation needs to go. I believe it is the most important question you can ask in every business setting as soon as the meeting begins. You will set the stage and walk away knowing if you met their expectations. This was a nugget of sales wisdom I didn't learn until my fifties.

35

When You Get A "No" ... Ask "Why"

ONE OF THE MOST important lessons I learned early on in baseball is that you are not going to get a hit every time up to bat. In fact, most of the time, a baseball swing results in an out. After failure, I would sit in the dugout trying to figure out what I did wrong my last at bat and how I could correct my next plate appearance. By learning from failures, I hoped to have better success the next time at the plate.

The same self-evaluation principles in baseball can be applied to sales. Everyone will get a "no" in sales. The key to becoming better is to find out why your prospective client said "no". So, after hearing "no", I would often inquire of my prospect; "I appreciate your frankness and honesty today. We're always looking for ways to improve. We want to become better and learn how our company might excel. Would you mind telling me, why you decided not to conduct business with us? That would really be helpful."

This may put them in an uncomfortable position if they're just making an excuse to get rid of you. Or you just might uncover the "real" objection which is insightful. Sometimes, just making a "change" bothers people and they don't want to be bothered with hearing about anything new. It's like every grandmother on "hair day"; it can be overwhelming to handle another chore on the same day as the beauty shop appointment. The patent answer if they're making an excuse is, "I'm just very busy right now." If they happen to give you a viable reason, it's to your advantage, because now you know exactly what you must overcome in the future.

Be sure to document every "no" and keep a list as to why you are being rejected and see if there is a pattern that can be corrected internally. Again, you are telling the client, "We became a great company, because we are continually looking for ways to improve and your input would be helpful." "No's" can be a good thing when used to find ways to enhance your game.

36

Be Bold And "Habla" With Confidence

IN 1979 I WAS SELECTED to represent the United States in the Intercontinental Baseball Cup played in Havana, Cuba. We were the first American baseball team that had played in Cuba since the revolution in 1959. It was an exceptional trip that I wrote about in my book, *Just A Phone Call Away*. The trip to Cuba was a real eye opener that helped me appreciate freedom and our great country. It was an honor representing America and when they played the Star-Spangled Banner before the game, we all sang loudly and proudly. Even many Cuban fans sang along with us.

We had some exceptional college players like Joe Carter, Terry Francona, Don Slaught and Ken Daley. But we were up against the best in the world and all the other countries were playing their older professionals including the Cuban team.

The night we played Cuba it was in front of 50,000 fans

in the Estadio Latinoamericana Stadium in Havana. I was warming up our starting pitcher, Ken Daley, in front of all the fans. Oddly in Latin ball parks, you warm up the pitcher directly in front of your dugout between home plate and first base. So, I was right next to the wall, about where the batters on-deck circle is situated.

In a flash, every fan in the ball park began to holler, "Fidel, Fidel, Fidel." As I looked up in the stands at the commotion, here comes El Comandante Fidel Castro walking down the aisle right towards me. I couldn't believe it when he sat down not more than twelve feet from me.

A bold thought came over me. Remembering I had surprisingly passed two semesters worth of Spanish at Vanderbilt left me beaming with confidence. Of course, I had never had a conversation with anyone of Hispanic descent and I was about to attempt my first conversation with the supreme leader of Cuba. Castro wearing his military outfit and sporting a cigar was a little bit intimidating as I pondered my introductory words.

There comes a point in time when you must be bold and "habla" and now was the time for me to speak, "Hola senor Castro". I slowly entered his space as two armed guards pointed their RPK soviet made machine guns in my direction. "Como esta el general?" Bingo! Fidel stood up, greeted me, welcomed me to Cuba and then walked down the steps to shake my hand.

It was probably not a good diplomatic move on my part for

the people of Cuba nor for our CIA, but I was just wanting to meet the guy. Adding to the moment, the fans were crazily cheering "USA", while Fidel Castro walked into our dugout and shook all the American players hands. It would be years later until I was informed of exactly how poorly my Spanish sounded conversing with the most recognized communist leader in the world whose native language was Spanish. At the time I didn't care because it was time to be bold and speak.

There will be times when you are required to make a sales presentation and you are not 100% sure of your talents. Be bold and speak with confidence. Some opportunities will never cross your path again. I'd rather regret that I did a poor job speaking than to regret that I never tried to speak at all.

37

Do Whatever It Takes To Win If It Is Legal, Moral and Makes Sense

IF YOU WANT TO SUCCEED you must be willing to do whatever it takes to be a winner. Losing is not an alternative lifestyle so all extra work is welcomed, necessary and required. Of course, you must not sacrifice either your faith or your family to win so the boundaries should be set at legal, moral and if it makes sense. You can run everything you need to do through these three grids and determine the work, the sacrifice, and the commitment it takes to be a winner.

Allow me to share a story when I was committed to win at all costs. Every day at the Los Angeles Dodger Spring practices in 1983, the coaches would rotate the players to different fields to work on different aspects of the game. Whistles would blow throughout the practice and the coaches expected and demanded that the players sprint to each field to begin the next station drill. My run consisted of me toting my Worth catching bag on my shoulder. It not only secured all my catching gear, but usually consisted of a third base glove; a first base glove; an outfield glove and at least three bats. My point here is that it was heavy, real heavy, especially when you were expected to lug it over your shoulders and jog to the next field. Catchers carrying similar weight were not expected to sprint to the next station, so a steady trot was acceptable.

This particular spring day, I glanced over my left shoulder and the wiry, high strung Coach Terry Collins (TC as we called him) approached me with a challenge. When I initially met Terry a season earlier in the California League, my first thoughts were, "This guy is too dang hyper even for me. He is wide open all the time."

Early in his coaching career, he was aggressive; assertive; feisty; and above all else cocky! Yet he was highly likeable and a favorite coach of mine. Terry was loyal to his players, and he loved the Dodgers. If Lasorda could have looked past his plate of lasagna, he would have recognized Terry Collins was his best choice for third base coach. I would have driven through hell with my window down to please a guy like Collins, whom I greatly admired! So, his upcoming challenge would be accepted!

Terry ran up alongside me and confidently boasted out so all could hear, "Madison, if I outrun you to the next field everyone on the team is going to have to run extra." Terry was carrying a Fungo bat and he was built like the green clay humanoid Gumby. I was carrying my heavy catching bag when we both took off wide-open in a 100-yard foot race.

It didn't take me long, maybe fifteen yards into the race, to realize Terry was about to get the best of me. So, I needed a plan to change the outcome of this race. For some reason, I crazily slung my Dodger blue catcher's bag over my shoulder and hurled it in the direction of TC's next stride, right at his feet. It was the perfect toss and a military sniper from a hundred yards away could not have catapulted TC in the air much higher. TC landed "all ass's and elbows" after doing what appeared to be a complete flip. His uniform had grass stains covering his entire right side. Terry did not like to get his uniform dirty, especially in this embarrassing way.

He came up cussing and hollering at me," What the hell are you doing?" I was laughing all the way to the next dugout and hollering, "I'm winning this race! I'm winning this race!" Terry always appreciated me after that and from that day forward admired my competitive nature. Being willing to win at all costs, would pay off for me when I played for him in the 1983 season in San Antonio, TX.

38

Run Through The Minefields
As Fast As You Can

As a young boy, I watched a movie with my father called "The Dirty Dozen". It was a war movie built around a bunch of misfits parachuting behind the German enemy lines and was loaded with acting talent; Donald Sutherland, Telly Savalas, Ernest Borgnine, Lee Marvin, Charles Bronson, and George Kennedy to name a few.

One celebrity actor in the movie was the great Cleveland Brown running back Jim Brown. In 2002 Jim was named the greatest player in the history of the NFL. Add to his recognition that EPSN recently named him the greatest player in college history. Certainly, he was an exceptional football player; he was big, tough, and very fast. His notoriety as a someone who could run landed him this role.

There was a scene in the movie where Jim Brown ran as fast as he could through a minefield to help complete the mission.

They portrayed it a little hokey and highly over exaggerated Jim Brown's athletic ability and speed. The movie showed him stepping on the mine and then running away with lightning speed before the mine blew off his leg. Yes, it was far-fetched, but made for an interesting movie scene.

We also step on mines in sales. Unlike Jim Brown however, there will be times when "blowing up" is unavoidable. You're not going to be able to outrun those failures. It won't hurt long, and you can recover, especially if you don't take it personally. To prevent it from becoming crippling, always face the bombs head on with grace and humility.

Answering challenging questions can be like stepping on mines. The question you are addressing might make you feel uncomfortable. In other words, when someone asks a tough question, even an unflattering one, don't avoid it. Give them your best answer with transparency and truth even if it hurts. This is a great test of your character and humility. You will find that by being direct and addressing their concern or issue will minimize the damage and gain his/her respect.

Always answer someone's question of concern immediately and then follow up with your own question, "Did I answer your question satisfactorily?" You will never make a sale if your prospect's questions go unanswered. Their unanswered questions create hesitancy and a lack of commitment from them in the sales process. No different than mines still out in front of you, unanswered questions should be addressed. Embrace the potential explosion, answer the question and anticipate the next question! The fallout from your truthful responses will never be as bad as you fear. You will walk away standing up.

39

Make Sure You Understand The Question

IF THERE EVER WAS a "hairy" predicament in sales for me, this is it. One season of life, maybe thirty plus years ago, I sold insurance to a company in Toone, TN. This particular company was a manufacturer of expendable infrared air counter-measures and other defense products. The employees at the plant made flare decoys for the Navy, so it was a highly volatile production environment. They warned us that just wearing the wrong kind of clothing might cause a spark that could cause an explosion.

Thus, we were very nervous entering the plant. Employees would walk in to see us wearing Darth Vader looking suits … hands shaking when they lit a cigarette in the lunch room … and identifying their job description as "powder mixers". Adding to our anxiety, we were offering a new unproven product. Aflac was making available a brand-new Hospital Indemnity plan and we were the first agents to offer it in the state of Tennessee. So, my great friend, Steve Steinhauer and I headed to the other side of Jackson, TN with high expectations to enroll new policyholders. Several months after a successful enrollment in the plant, our "headache" began. After receiving a phone call from the head of Human Resources, I called Steve.

"Steve, hey I just received a phone call from the head of HR in Toone."

"Yea, what's up?"

"Well, it appears that they had an employee that went into the hospital in Jackson for seven days and he filed a claim with Aflac … and Aflac denied the claim. They said he had a pre-existing condition."

Steve was quiet at first, "Ok, what's that got to do with me?"

I hated to answer him, "Tommy says he was sitting beside you when you talked with this guy. He said he heard the conversation, and you told the man he could have the hospital indemnity policy. Evidently the man told you he had something going on with his health and you still enrolled him."

Steve was heightened now, "What, that's crazy! You know I would never do anything like that."

"I know … I know, I hear you but let me ask you a question. Do you know what Renal Failure is?"

Steve paused on the other end of the line, "Does it have something to do with either your eye or your bottom … you know your Renal?"

I knew this is where we got off the rails, "Well, I think that's where we have a problem. See your Renal is not your eye or your bottom. Renal Failure is the same as kidney disease."

There was a pause on the line as Steve was looking for some reassurance, "And what did you think it was when you first heard about Renal Failure?"

"I thought it had something to do with your eye or your bottom, too. I had to look it up." "See", Steve stated, "So what are we going to do", as we both looked for a way out of a problem brought on innocently with honorable intentions?

I was not sure what to do, "I don't think we have much choice, but to pay the man. I'm going to get $400, which I don't have, and you are going to come up with $300, which you don't have, and we're going to drive to Toone and sit down with this fellow and see if we can make him happy, by paying him what the hospital plan would have paid him."

"I don't have any money?"

"I don't either, but we have to make this right." AND WE DID!

What went wrong to put us in this "uncomfortable" predicament? First of all, we had very limited if any training from our company on the new product. With a little training, we would have linked kidney disease with Renal Failure. Next, we were offering a hospital indemnity plan that had unfamiliar health questions. The health question that stumped both Steve and I involved Kidney Failure. On the application, the actual question read, "Have you or anyone to be covered every had kidney failure?" It never mentioned the word Renal Disease or Renal Failure. Yes, we should have known the two were linked, but we honestly didn't know that word.

Finally, we failed to understand a critical qualifying question. When asked "Have you ever had any health problems? He answered, "I've had Renal Failure." "Well, no problem. Renal Failure is not listed on the application so you're good to go. Sign right here please!" We were being truthful, in our ignorance.

Through our continuous improvement efforts, within six months of our mistake, Aflac added the words, "Renal Disease and Renal Failure" to the application. Obviously, there were some other agents that thought it had something to do with your back end, too. Taking a page from the original "Bad News Bears" classic film, never "ass-u-me".

If your prospect makes a statement that is not 100% clear to you, then be sure to obtain clarification. Before you move forward, be completely clear as to the exact question and the response. Try something like this, "I want to make sure I understood what you are stating," and then repeat exactly what you thought you heard followed by, "Is this correct?" If yes, proceed with your direct answer to their question. I like to then follow up with this remark, "Did that answer your question?" or "Do I understand that correctly?"

You don't want to make the same mistake we made ... a mistake that was innocently made but could have been prevented with the right follow up questions.

40

Reintroduce Your Self Again And Again

I HAVE A GOOD FRIEND in Nashville, TN, H. Lee Barfield. Lee is a retired prominent attorney at Bass Berry and Sims. He is politically active in education for the underserved and is always in the middle of a worthy cause. He might be one of the finest men I've ever met. Lee's known for a lot of good things, but he might be most famous in Nashville for the introduction.

I've known Lee for some thirty-five years, but that doesn't matter when it comes to greeting Lee after you haven't seen him in a while. Every time Lee sees you, regardless of the number of times, he always extends his hand and says, "Lee Barfield, how you are doing Scotti."

"Lee, I know who you are."

If you can ask anyone in Nashville or along 30A, Lee will always greet you by stating his name. It doesn't matter how long he's known you. The running joke in his family comes from his wife Mary, "Heck, when Lee wakes up in the morning beside me, he introduces himself."

So how did this greeting habit begin with Lee? He told me it began in 1971 when he greeted Winfield Dunn, the Governor of Tennessee. Governor Dunn was the first Republican governor in fifty years and Lee was attending an event where he would meet Governor Dunn.

"I walked up to the Governor and said, 'Hello Governor, I'm Lee Barfield.' The Governor paused and greeted me with a more personal response, 'Lee, I can't thank you enough for introducing yourself to me. I know who you are, but there are so many people I meet that I just don't remember their names and as Governor, people are always coming up to me and saying, 'Governor, hello, do you remember me?' And of course, I don't know them or remember them and it's so embarrassing for me. You make it a lot easier on me by introducing yourself. Thank you!'"

So, Lee recognized how important it was to continually repeat your name when you meet someone, and he passed it on to me. When you think about it, that's a good thing. It takes the pressure off the person you're greeting when they don't remember your name. How often do you forget someone's name when you see them and feel so awkward? You feel especially discomfited when they call you by your name. Lee not only calls you by your name, he re-states his name to you to avoid any uncomfortable situation on your part.

I find this greeting strategy in sales or life in general to be brilliant and I have used it religiously. If you keep doing this consistently, I can promise you the other person will remember your name much quicker. It won't be long before they call your name out before you reach them. Maybe you can't do it every time like Lee does, but give it a try and it will become a good habit for you to practice in all areas of introductions.

41

Don't Just Kill To Kill Or Sell To Sell

WHEN I WAS NINE YEARS OLD, I received a Daisy Red Rider BB gun from Santa Claus ... yea just like the kid in the movie, *A Christmas Story*. I didn't "shoot my eye out" like Ralphie Parker thought he did, but Ralphie didn't have to eat what he killed.

As my story goes, a couple of days after Christmas, I'm in the backyard with my weapon of choice when I spotted several birds across the yard. I focused on a Blue Jay through the cross hairs, and followed the BB across the yard after I pulled the trigger. It was a lucky shot when I killed the Blue Jay. It was not so lucky for me when I heard a knock on the window coming from the house.

I looked up to see my father banging on the bathroom window and motioning me to do something. Dad had witnessed my successful hunt. He raised the window and hollered, "Hey bring that dead Blue Jay in the house."

I was kind of alarmed and not quite sure where this was heading. With the Blue Jay in hand, I walked into the kitchen where Dad was resting against the sink, "Son, let me tell you something about using a gun and hunting. We don't just kill to kill. If you kill something, you're going to eat it. So, tonight we're having Chicken fried steak. You're going to have Chicken fried Blue Jay."

As ordered, I cleaned the bird as best I could and brought it back into the house. It didn't look too appetizing even with all its feathers gone. That night at the dinner table, there was snickering coming from my family as they saw the cooked Blue Jay on my plate; bird legs pointing straight upwards. I can promise you that Blue Jay doesn't taste like chicken.

It was certainly an impactful moment for me. For the rest of my life, every time I hunt, I know I should eat what I kill. I will never shoot at a Blue Jay again.

I tell you this because this same philosophy applies in selling. People don't need to buy something from you unless they really need it. You don't just kill to kill, and you don't just sell to sell. It's great to make money, but don't try to make money selling something to someone they don't really need. That gives every salesperson a bad name and is just bad "karma". Be honorable. Find a product you believe in and then sell it to someone that really needs your product. Often, it's better to walk away and pass the sale up if your prospect doesn't need what you're offering. If someone buys something from you that they don't need, it will probably leave a bad taste in their mouth ... kind of like Blue Jay.

42

Be Professionally Consistent And Professionally Persistent

Looking back at my baseball career, I cherish the minor leagues even more than the "Big Leagues". I think it's because of the journey, the effort and the personal experience put into chasing the dream rather than acquiring the dream. I knew it might take some time before I made it and was willing to pay the necessary price to make it. I spent five years in the minor leagues chasing my dream before the Detroit Tigers called me up. But that isn't the norm when it comes to most minor league players trying to make it.

First to third round draft picks usually average 3-4 years in the minor leagues, but should be in AAA by the 4th year or close to it. If not, they send them home. Later round draft picks, maybe the 15th round or later, are not given that much grace. If they spend three years at the same level in the minor leagues, they will be released and sent home. Very few players continue to play after four years and even fewer make it to the Big Leagues in the fifth year or longer.

I traveled the same persistent road and put in my time in the business world. For example, it took ten years before one company did business with me. During those years, I would continue to "drip" my name, my company, or my product about once every 45 to 60 days with a typed letter or hand-written note. This was the pre-email era. I stopped by for a personal visit, just to say hello, about every two months. It paid off to be consistent and persistent.

It's critical to follow back up with early sales opportunities. If you don't, you open the door for the competition. Opportunities are never lost … someone will take the ones you miss when you don't follow up.

In today's environment, it will feel annoying to receive an email from a salesperson every two weeks. You receive so much junk mail in your business folder, so they surely don't need your email. It drives me crazy when I buy a service or product, give them my email and the company begins to email a notification on something they are selling every day. I immediately stop all correspondence. Once a month would be plenty.

This is a very impersonal way of reaching out to a potential customer. If emailing is your sales method of "dripping" your name, you're doing nothing more than being a part of the annoying spam emails they receive daily.

Instead, consistently reach out with minimal emails

balanced with some handwritten letters or notes, as well as the occasional personal visit. This form of professional "drip" enhances your opportunity to close the deal. The reason that you always call back your "no's" on a professionally consistent basis is because it works.

Sometimes when people say "no", your adversary has been poor timing. Something might be going on in their life that impedes their ability to make any type of decision. So, keep your list of "no's" and maybe seven to eight weeks out when you're blowing and going, re-engage the "no". Try something like this in a call or personal visit, "Hey there, I hope this finds you well. It has been some time since we last spoke and I really appreciated your time with me earlier. I am following up to see if maybe things have changed at your company. We have continued to improve our product and services and I hope we can have some conversation in the near future."

If you are not willing to re-engage your "no's", sales are not for you. You must be committed to put the time in for as long as it takes. If you're professionally consistent and professionally persistent, you will build a successful business career in sales over time.

43

What Is Your Economic Value?

WHAT ARE YOU actually worth to your company as a salesperson? Have you ever thought about that? There are times in sales you will get paid what you think you are worth. Then other times, your ego has inflated your true value to your company, and you feel like you are underpaid. I'm asking you how much do you think you are worth in your current sales role? There is a value your company places on your effort and more than likely it's less than what you're getting paid. And it should be because the company must turn a profit.

Most of the time when I listen to someone new in the sales industry talk about their pay, they always state, "I should be making more. They are not paying me what I'm worth." This problem is easy to solve. If you can sell one widget, you can sell another, so if you're not happy with your pay, find another sales opportunity. Companies are always looking for good salespeople, so sales jobs are easy to find.

I used to think the same way early in my insurance career, during the same time I was trying to be a baseball player. And then I learned a valuable lesson from Donald Fehr, the current Executive Director of the National Hockey League Players Association.

I first met Don when I served as the player representative for the Kansas City Royals in 1988. He served as the director of the Major League Baseball Players Association from 1983 to 2009. It was during this time I was coerced into the player rep position for the Royals after George Brett nominated me in a team meeting, "Does anybody else on our team have a degree from Vanderbilt?" The next thing I knew we were headed to play the Yankees and as the new player representative, I was to meet with Mr. Fehr at the players association offices in uptown New York.

It was a very contentious time in professional baseball and the owners were expecting the players to strike by next season. I didn't favor that course of action and I questioned Don as to why we would strike, "Don, I don't think striking is a good idea. They can call up minor league players and eventually this might negatively affect our salaries. You can't blame the owners … they have the risk and must turn a profit".

Don calmly looked out the window of the Manhattan offices and said, "Do you know what determines the economic value of a player, how you determine your salary?"

I wasn't sure what the exact answer was, yet I did hope to

appear somewhat intelligent, "How good you are at doing something?"

Don smiled, "Close … there is a little more to it than that. What determines someone's value is three-fold, 1) The demand for what you do 2) Your ability to do something well 3) The difficulty in replacing you with someone else."

What a profound way to understand just how much you should make selling whatever it is you sell. Think about what Donald Fehr told me? You are going to be paid well if your product or service is highly sought after by the consumer; you sell your product or service better than anyone else in the industry; and it is nearly impossible to replace someone of your talents. I hope you take heed to Don's wisdom explaining how you determine what your economic value should be in your sales role going forward. Apply these three measures to your sales position and see where you stand.

44

Your Opportunity Horizon Changes

IN 1989 I WAS with the Cincinnati Reds in Spring Training and my manager was the legendary Pete Rose. I know most everyone knows the story of his lifetime banishment from baseball. But every player who played for Pete loved him; me being one of them. Pete was a player's manager meaning he looked out for the best interest of his players. And above all else, Pete wanted to win, and I was all about that, too.

I remember the time Kal Daniels, was in a contract dispute with the team. Marge Schott, the Reds owner, agreed to settle the dispute through a coin flip rather than pay attorneys in an arbitration hearing. Marge called heads, but the coin came up tails, so Daniels was paid his requested $325,000. Pete was so excited when Daniels came back into the locker room, "Kal that's awesome you called tails and won. You know tails comes up more often than heads."

I played well during spring camp in 1989 and could've made the Reds Major League club out of Spring Training. Instead, Pete called me in his office about four days before camp broke and told me that they were sending me back to Triple A. When I walked in the room, Murray Cook, the General Manager, was sitting behind the desk and Pete was lounging back in a chair beside my seat.

The conversation went something like this as Pete bit his fingernail and then began, "Scrapper, have a seat…man you had a great spring, but we need to send you back to Triple A. Thank you for all the hard work you gave me this spring."

I'm thinking, 'That's it … after all my hard work?' I was crushed to hear those disheartening words and my opportunity horizon was completely shut. Reality is … I was not going to make the Cincinnati Reds team out of Spring Training. Yea, it was cool that Pete called me "Scrapper". The bottom line, I was headed back to the minor leagues. At that moment in time, all the hard work put into my dream seemed like a waste of time. I was thinking 'what good had it done me to work so hard' as I was grasping for the right response?

I had nothing to lose talking to arguably the greatest baseball player of all time, "Pete, man … you didn't give me a chance to make this club. I had a great spring camp and hit as good as anyone. You know I out hustled everyone on this team. No body worked harder than me to make this club. Pete, I'm just like you. I love the game … I dedicated my life to baseball … I'm the first one on the field and the last one to leave."

Pete continued to stare at me when I came to my closing thought, "Pete, I should've made this club, but you really didn't know anything about me. Now you do! Will you make a promise to me right now, that during the season, if a player goes down and you need a hitter, and I'm hitting well in Nashville, you'll call me up?"

I often wondered if Pete saw a little of his inner drive in me when he responded. He smiled, paused for a moment, and said, "If I need a hitter and you're doing good, you'll get the call." And Pete Rose was good to his word that summer … I was the first player called up from the minor leagues.

My opportunity horizon changed during the course of the season. When Chris Sabo, the Reds third baseman went down with a season ending injury, Pete called me up to play third base for the Reds, even though I was playing right field and first base in Triple A Nashville. If you make good numbers and do your job, they will find you a place to play.

Time has the ability to change the "no" to a "yes". Every day your opportunity horizon can change if you continue to do the work. Life is constantly on the move. Situations and circumstances change with a prospective customer you previously pursued. You'll never know the situation has changed unless you're calling them back on a persistent basis. Just as your product and company continues to change, so do the customer's needs over time.

For example, maybe your pricing changed, or your delivery model has improved. By writing down why they initially said "no" in the first place, you'll know how to fulfill their need when you call back again. You'll never know you've reached a "yes" until you're willing to stick with it and walk back into your opportunity horizon.

45

Just Outwork Everyone

SEVERAL TIMES during my career I have been asked by young men and women entering the sales profession, "What is the one tip you can give me that will help my career?"

My prevailing answer was always, "Out work everyone in your company and out work all your competition." Most of the time they didn't want to hear that unsettling answer. They were looking for something magical; something else to advance their careers that didn't involve more effort, extra hours, sacrifice, and missing sleep. They were looking for a shortcut, an easy way to success.

There are no shortcuts when it comes to work. I've always believed if you outworked everyone, you're going to be better than 95% of the field. The rest of the journey to the top is a dogfight. When you think about it, the one resource that everyone has, the one consistent asset that puts everyone on level ground, is time. Your advantage is derived as to what you do with your time compared to others. You have a good idea if you're personally making the most of each day. If you must ask yourself, "Am I using my time wisely?" Then, there's a pretty good chance you're not.

Work harder than the person looking back at you in the mirror. Push yourself each and every day to be superior in your "walk and talk". Successful sales are about optimizing every moment you are given to become better than you were the day before.

Everyone has the chance to give 100% effort, 100% of the time. If you can't do that then you need to find a profession outside of sales. Talent may vary, but time and effort are the great equalizer. I've found at times that those with exceptional natural talents usually don't have the same exceptional work ethic as others operating with far less ability.

Contrary to the above finding, there were a couple of exceptions that I had the privilege of personally witnessing when I played ball. One case in point was Hall of Famer, George Brett. George was an absolute super star player, and his work habits were second to none. George combined his incredible talents at the plate, as a Hall of Fame hitter, with dedicated work effort every day. He did whatever it took to stay great often taking extra batting practice in the batting cages long into the day. There were other exceptionally talented players that I saw work extra hard. Players like Cal Ripkin Jr., Tony

Gwynn, Don Mattingly, Alan Trammell and Bo Jackson all had exceptional natural ability, but they worked as hard as the player trying to make it with average talent.

Everyone wants to live on top of the mountain, but your character and your growth in life occurs while climbing. Be willing to take advantage of each precious hour working like it's your last moment in time. God gives everyone twenty-four hours a day. Once it's gone, you can't get it back. You don't get a re-do on time and you don't get a re-do on effort. So, wake up every day committed to do the work necessary to become exceptional in your field.

46

The Early Bird Buys Breakfast

IT'S IMPORTANT to spend money to make money. This often means you might be taking a prospective client out to eat somewhere. Early in your career, extra money for "wining and dining" is hard to find. You're just getting started and money is tight. I suggest you treat your guest to breakfast. You'll always find that buying breakfast will not be near as expensive as either lunch or dinner. Besides, you can tell how serious a person is about your business relationship if they join you for breakfast.

You can also tell if they are a "go getter". The early bird does get the worm and someone who is a morning person is probably an over achiever. Breakfast will be a better time of the day for them considering new ideas and making your acquaintance for the first time.

If you can't get them to join you for breakfast, take the breakfast to them. Early in my career, I woke up very early and would hold my baseball workouts at the Vanderbilt facilities before the sun came up. Upon completion, around 7:15AM, I'd put a tie on and begin calling on small businesses with either bagels or Krispy Kreme doughnuts in hand. My breakfast meeting began when I entered their front door, "Good morning, I was wondering if you might have some coffee around here ... I brought the doughnuts."

Most of the time, the person who greets you in a small business early in the morning is the owner. If they opened the doors early, I always found they would take time with a salesperson that came calling just as early, especially one who brought hot Krispy Kreme Doughnuts.

47

Wolves Have Better Table Manners

I CANNOT PREACH enough about the importance of good table manners. There is nothing that directly demonstrates your character, your upbringing, and your pedigree more than how you hold a fork and carry yourself around a meal. I don't place too much emphasis on confusing your salad fork from your desert fork. But your good manners at a meal will assure that your guest and your host are comfortable. If you get this wrong in front of a prospective client, it could turn out to be the reason why they choose not to do business.

I hope the following story demonstrates the importance of manners. I once had a farm in Dadeville, AL and I was always entertaining guests. My children and my nephews would come quite often, and I would prepare steaks at least one night during their visit. One week in early December, my daughter, Tori, had invited some classmates from the University of Alabama and my nephew Clifford, would bring his cadet classmates from West Point a few days later. Both groups were coming in to get some R&R.

Tori informed me that her five friends were honor students and all very bright in the classroom. In fact, they were some of the best honor students The University of Alabama had to offer. They were extremely well behaved, courteous, yet somewhat reserved. They were quite content riding on golf carts and taking in the scenic sights on the farm. When it was time to eat, I was somewhat taken back.

I was expecting model college students to have better manners, but found out differently. Only one in the group knew how to properly hold a fork and knife to cut their steak. No one knew how to pass the food dishes around the table counterclockwise. They just stood up and reached whatever they needed for their meal. Some chewed with their mouths open; some used their fingers as the backstop for shoveling food on their forks and worst of all, they licked every finger at the table. They weren't much for helping clean the table after dinner either.

While cleaning the dishes, Tori came up to me and acknowledged their 'wolf like manners'. "Dad, I've never really eaten with them before. Kinda bad huh?" They were not invited back.

Then on the other hand, the graduates from The United States Military Academy arrived a day later. They were not content with riding golf carts. In fact, they drove my four wheelers into the ground; they shot guns all over the wooded property; they consumed beer like it was air. Also, they drove their trucks through the planted fields and even got their trucks stuck in the muddiest spots on the property. Then they came to dinner.

They had exemplary manners. They waited until everyone was seated before the first person took a bite. Of course, they began by blessing the food. They cut their meat correctly, chewed with their mouths closed and properly passed the food at the table. It was so enjoyable to dine with gentlemen. I was so impressed with each of them I asked, "Clifford, man ... ya'll have really good table manners. Do you have an etiquette class at West Point?"

"Yea, Uncle Scotti, we have a mandatory class everyone must take on table manners and proper etiquette in public. We all sit down together at West Point and wait to eat at the same time. It's community style so, we learn how to pass the food and drink around to the right. They preach if you're going to be an officer, you need to have manners and be a gentleman, too."

I thought to myself, why don't all Universities make students take an etiquette class? After all, once they're graduates, they represent the University when they're dining with someone. Who cares how smart they are ... if they eat like wolves, you tend to overlook their other good qualities. A prospect might certainly overlook your product if you have poor manners. If you can practice the following tips on manners, you will be way ahead of most Gen Y, Millenial's and Gen Z today.

Table Manner DO'S

- Sit properly (and straight) in your chair.
- Place your napkin on your lap.
- Wait until everyone is seated before starting to eat.
- Wait for your host or hostess to be seated.
- Watch others, or ask, if you're not sure how to eat something.
- Ask someone to please pass the food (counter clockwise) rather than reach across the table.
- You can eat chicken with your fingers.
- Chew with your mouth closed.
- Don't talk with your mouth full.
- Say "may I please be excused" before leaving the table.
- Put the butter on your butter plate, not on your bread when it's passed.
- Pass the salt and pepper at the same time.
- Cut your food with a knife, even your large leaves on your salad.

Table Manner DON'TS

- Don't ask for seconds before others have had firsts.
- Don't take more than your fair share your first serving.
- Don't overload your fork.

- Don't be the first to finish eating.
- Don't gobble your food, it's not a race.
- Don't show up at a business luncheon starving.
- Don't lick your fingers in a public setting.
- Don't push your plate away when finished.
- Don't stack your plates when you're cleaning up.
- Don't eat everything on your plate. Leave a little bit for the purpose of etiquette.

48

Be Willing To Ask For The Order

ONE OF THE HARDEST items of business in your sales career is to be willing to ask for the order. There will come a time when you have delivered all the insight and information you've been asked about your product and your company. Your prospect has been courted for some time and they are a person in the company that can say, "yes". Now it's time for you, with complete confidence, to ask them to do business with you.

"Asking for the order" can be quite difficult early in the life of a salesperson. Yet, it's a necessary criterion in your sales career if you are to experience any sales success. Then the question becomes, "just how do you ask?" What is the best way to ask for their business?

During my thirty-five years in sales, I have approached the "close" hundreds of times. It has varied based on the personality of the prospect, the location of your meeting and the mood of your prospective client. I settled on one question after years of trial and error. Thus, I would begin the conversation by stating, "I think we have delivered to you everything you have asked of us regarding our products and services, as well as our company; is there any reason you can think of as to why you would not want to do business with us?" This question either moves the conversation to close or delivers to you any rebuttal that needs to be addressed before obtaining their business.

Looking back in life, my first important close would determine whether or not I was going to graduate from Vanderbilt. I had just finished my first season of minor league baseball with the Minnesota Twins. I was the second catcher selected in the draft in 1980; a third-round draft pick; first team All-American and player of the year in the Southeastern Conference. My agent was Robert Fraley, a great man of integrity and a successful sports agent to the stars, especially high-profile coaches. He had an extraordinary range of sports celebrities he represented. I was his first client. Robert would later tragically die in a plane crash with Payne Stewart in the plains of South Dakota on October 25, 1999.

So, with some athletic success and the most admired up and coming agent in the country, I knew I was looking at a big payday. Instead, I signed for $12,000. The Twins and owner Calvin Griffith were the cheapest team in baseball. Now, four months later and with no money, I needed a plan to finish college and it wasn't an instate Junior College. It was Vanderbilt, so the tuition was out of my reach. I was nine hours short of graduating and would have to meet with the Vanderbilt Athletic Director, Roy Kramer, and ask him if the athletic department would pay for my last nine hours of college.

I walked in to McGugin Center and sat down in front of Coach Kramer, "Good morning, Coach, how are you and Ms. Sara Jo doing?" Sara Jo was coach's wife, and she was the woman behind the curtain. She was vibrant, a cheerleader of sorts and always funny. Coach shuffled in his chair, "We are both doing well Scotti. I hope you had a good summer of baseball. So, what can I do for you?"

I just nodded my head, 'yes sir' to the baseball question, as I was deep in thought as to what next to say? It was now the beginning of September and classes at Vanderbilt were already a week in progress. My hands were sweaty as I cleared my throat. I looked across the desk at the man before me that was larger than life and he was all of that. Coach Roy Kramer was a legend in Michigan High School football as well as in the college ranks. He'd won championships everywhere he coached. Now, he was rebuilding the Athletic programs at Vanderbilt. He would later leave the university to become the Commissioner of the Southeastern Conference and was the visionary and creator of the Bowl Championship Series in NCAA football. This is the man sitting before me that I was about to ask for the order.

"Coach, I need your help. I'm nine hours short of graduating and I was hoping you could find a way to help me pay for school."

Coach Kramer sat back in his chair, and I could see his mind running somewhere other than to the Athletic Department checkbook, "Well Scotti, lots of college players have to go back and complete their degrees. We've already fulfilled our responsibility to you regarding college paying for four years of school. You don't have any more eligibility left and have signed a professional contract."

I was hoping for a little different answer; maybe along the lines of, "nine hours is nothing, we can help". I began to think, what was I going to say now, because if I were going to complete my college degree, it was now or never? I really wanted that Vanderbilt degree.

I began to tell Coach that I'd made good grades all four years and the nine hours I needed to graduate were classes in my business major that were only offered after 3:00PM each semester. It was impossible for me to take them since I was playing both football and baseball at Vandy.

Coach kept going back to his foundational reply, "Scotti, we just believe we've fulfilled our duty to you paying for four years' worth of college."

I knew I wasn't getting anywhere, and time was running out. I was backed into a corner and had everything to lose. I thought to myself, *this is it* as I searched for the words, "Coach, wouldn't it be a tragedy if Vanderbilt's very first, First Team All American in baseball didn't graduate?"

I just stared at him and never blinked. Coach sat deeper in thought in his chair as I felt all the air leave the room, "Well, Sara Jo always liked you. You were her favorite player. Go ahead and see John Shafer and work something out with him."

I shook Coach Kramer's hand and gratefully thanked him. I walked the hall and met Coach Shafer, the assistant AD, who had once played and coached baseball at Auburn. Coach Shafer not only agreed to pay for my tuition, Coach paid for some meals during the week and set me up in a dorm room, compliments of the Vanderbilt Athletic Department.

Looking back in my life, it was my most important 'ask' and if I hadn't met with Coach Kramer and asked for the order, I don't believe I'd have completed my Vanderbilt college degree.

49

The Art Of Story Telling

T HERE WILL BE TIMES when your prospective buyer just can't seem to find value in your product or service. There seems to be a stalemate and your efforts are to no avail. A good way to bring some interest and insight to your conversation is to use a story that relates to the situation at hand. The art of story telling has been around before the written word. Most people learn visually and when you can weave a story into the presentation, many times they can see it happening in their mind.

Many of the best salesmen and saleswomen are also, the best storytellers. Everyone can't be one, but if you are, then stay interesting and keep talking. Storytellers have a knack for diffusing a buyer's reservation through a situation or story. The story takes the prospect back into his or her past of a similar experience and demonstrates two points of importance: 1) We've helped other people just like you and 2) The storyteller is a real person and a nice person that can be trusted.

Good stories about life allow the prospective buyer to become relaxed and comfortable with the salesperson. These positive stories might be what some buyers need to hear to feel confident to move forward with a "yes". It certainly helps the prospect relate to you as a human being.

I once befriended one of the greatest storytellers that ever lived. There was a country comedian I occasionally saw while attending Vanderbilt by the name of Jerry Clower. Wikipedia Jerry Clower and it will tell his entire story. The country singer Jerry Reed, of "Smoky and the Bandit" fame, introduced us to each other. Clower wore big bright ruffled clothes, mostly red, and told real life stories about living in the country and funny stories about coon hunting, log trucks and eating at the dining room table with the Ledbetter family.

Jerry started out as a fertilizer salesman for the Mississippi Chemical Company in Yazoo City, Mississippi. He was so successful selling fertilizer that his company officials wanted to try and replicate his success. They couldn't because he was unique and told his life-experience stories from the heart to his customers. His stories were so genuine and warm hearted, that he started performing public speaking and soon found his way to the Grand Ole Opry, then on records and radio.

If you need to tell a story about a satisfied customer, you might start by stating, "That's a good question and reminds me of a story." Then proceed to tell your story. Don't embellish it; tell the truth, because your prospect just might think, "I'm going to fact check this person?" So, be ready to back your story up with the person who was the main character. If you can present a viable real-life story, it might take the uncomfortable edge off the prospect giving you a better chance of doing business and making the sale.

50

If You Get Knocked Down 7 Times, Get Up 8

An old Japanese saying encouraging a person to keep trying was used often by the great Zig Ziglar, "You don't drown falling into the water; you drown only if you stay there."

I was fortunate to have played college football in the Southeastern Conference. I would say it was a challenge to have been a quarterback for Vanderbilt from 1976 to 1979. During that three-year period, we were 2-9 each season ... 2 being the number of wins. When I did play, which was not often, I found myself lying on the artificial turf quite a few times during the game. Being tackled more than the normal quarterback taught me that when you get knocked down, when you fail, get right back up and be ready for the next play.

During the season, I would call my father on a Thursday night, "Dad, we had a great week of practice. We are going to beat Alabama this week." Then next week it was Georgia and the following week LSU, and I exercised the same confidence in an identical conversation the entire season. Dad always said, "Well son, I hope so."

As the games played out on Saturdays, we were very good for three quarters and every play I believed with all my heart that we would win. We might lose by 20 points, and I would go through the same mental check down the next week. In the middle of the week, I practiced every day believing we would win our next game…that's what you must do to survive and live hopeful. Always believe you are going to WIN!

In sales, getting a "no" is survivable. In life, a loss is survivable, too. You must believe you will be victorious the next time you try. And if you get a "no" again, you continue moving forward to play the next game, still believing that your next call will be a "yes".

What I learned early on is that you will fail a lot more than you succeed, which I did in college football. I can assure you in my illustrious football career, I was sacked more times behind the line of scrimmage than touchdown passes I completed. This experience carried over in sales and taught me how to get up when I got knocked down. You will fail; you will face some hardship. Don't walk into a sales call and expect it. Yet, deal with it when it happens. It becomes a complete failure only when you're not willing to get back up and try again. Remember, you only drown if you choose to stay under water. You only fail in life and in sales … if you don't try.

51

It's Better To Live Like A Prince For A Lifetime Than A King For A Moment

I COMPLETELY FAILED to live by this principle early in my life. When I was at the top of my game and had plenty of money coming in monthly, I felt like the windfall would last longer than it did. Many people go through life thinking that it's going to be tomorrow when they are going to change, really make a difference in their life. Tomorrow will be the day they wake up and begin to do exactly what they are supposed to do ... to change their life for the good. But then tomorrow comes and goes, and then the next day, and the next month and then actually years pass. Soon all the tomorrows have passed and the opportunity to make a positive difference in your life has also passed.

Oh, I was able to pay off debt and own our home, but more savings should have been set-aside by me for rainy days and retirement. I kept telling myself, 'I can set more money aside next year'. Unfortunately, next year never came and Aflac lost my top three clients in one terrible year. In essence, I lost 90% of my income in the course of that dreadful year. Thus, the opportunity to build a substantial savings was forever gone.

During the good times, I was able to live like a king for seven years, but never like a prince after the fall. It would have been wiser to plan on living like a prince in the beginning, which probably could have lasted for forty years.

I present to you this warning, so that you will take the time to follow a philosophy from someone like Dave Ramsey and his Financial Peace program. You must learn the importance of financial savings as a priority early in your sales career. By establishing a financial plan for life, you will use savings to build financial priorities like an emergency fund, set-aside three months income, pay off debt, pay the IRS and build a retirement account. The sooner you get this right, the less pressure you feel in sales. The longer you can stay out of debt, the easier it is to sell out of inspiration and not desperation. Choose to live like a prince for a lifetime!

52

Tis Far Better To Give Than To Sale

As I HAVE EMPHASIZED in this read, a sales career is very hard and not for everyone. Commissioned salespeople will find it to be even harder than a salesperson on a salary. The pressure to make a sale in order to live requires daily attention to maintain a healthy perspective. Some people are cut out for this line of work. Others who wear their feelings on their shirtsleeve or believe in participation trophies will never be a good salesperson. It takes a rare breed to be good in sales and it often requires giving more of your self, your time, and your resources than you imagined.

Even after looking back, there is no other career in the world I would consider other than commission sales. It is so exhilarating to "close a deal" and I find it to be just as rewarding as when I played a ball game, and we left the field victorious. What other career can reward you financially for your efforts where there is no ceiling on your income. I know of no other profession in life where your success is directly related to a combination of your personal effort, dedicated preparation and ultimately "God's favor". There is nothing like working for your self and working under the motto, "you eat what you kill."

If you follow some of my sales tips I laid out and attempt to become excellent in the "walk and talk" in all areas of your life, I am highly confident you can have a bright career. Your reward for effort, perseverance, professional persistence, humility and exercising wisdom will be more than just financial. You will experience enriched relationships and friendships that will be more valuable than the monetary resources you earn.

In sales, you can learn so much from a plethora of businesses. Yet, to reach greater heights of gratification, you need to have a heart for "giving". This is the ultimate achievement of reaching your highest calling. When friends refer to you as a giver ... a servant to others, you've arrived. By helping others reach their goals in life, your memorial service will be well attended by people who love you. There is no greater purpose in life than to give of one's self completely to a worthy ideal.

If there is only one "must" to take away from all my sales tips, learn to be a generous giver. Give of your time to help others. Be willing to give of your expertise to others in your profession who might just be getting started. Then every time you reap the blessings of successful sales, be willing to give to those less fortunate. When you share your financial blessings, it will be far more rewarding than any personal sales accomplishment. It's sure great to make a sale ... it's even greater when God can bless others through you.

Good luck and may God bless you as you live to perfect the "walk and talk" in your life and reach your highest possible attainable level in the life of a salesperson.

My Best,
SCOTTI MADISON

BONUS STORIES AND LESSONS

1

Friendships ... The Lasting Motivator

I BELIEVE there are three determining factors that motivate the psyche of all people to purchase something. A Buyer is either motivated to move on a decision because there is a favorable relationship involved or because they are either making money or saving money.

Ultimately in time, the buyer must make or save money even if there is a friendship involved. But it's a friendship or a friendly relationship that ignites the opportunity on the front end and it's what keeps it together when the walls are falling down… i.e., there is a product or service problem.

Creating friendships is one of the foundational principles in enhancing your "walk and talk". It will drive more sales than any other talent, skill, or attribute you possess. It will generate more quality time in front of your prospect than other sales techniques or talent. There is a biblical proverb known as the

Golden Rule "do unto others as you would have them do unto you." How do you want to be treated? Do you appreciate being treated like a friend? Well, so does your customer!

What are some actions you can take to enhance that "walk and talk" becoming a friend to everyone you call on?

1) Instead of just sending an email thanking someone for their time, which is better than nothing; consider going the extra mile and hand write them a note. Yes, this is "old school", and no one does this anymore. Yet, this thoughtful gesture and extra effort will set you apart from everyone else in your school; on your team; in your offices and in your industry. Before I landed Wal-Mart as an Aflac client, I had written probably a dozen notes or letters to my contact inside Wal-Mart over a five-year period. When Wal-Mart was ready to finally send Aflac a RFP on supplemental benefits, they requested that Scotti Madison be the servicing agent. To this day, I believe Wal-Mart was a blessing from God, but I'm also quite confident the personal handwritten letters helped the sales process.

2) Make the time to visit just as a friend and not a solicitation. Taking the time to personally visit someone is always time well spent. When someone personally takes the time to come and see you, how does that make you feel? Too many times a salesperson only reaches out with

a sales pitch. Stopping by to just say, "hello" is an important gesture in building a friendship and lasting business relationship.

3) Take an interest in their personal life and family. It's important that you understand your prospective client has a life, too. There is a family somewhere, which means they experience both the highs and lows of life dealing with family matters. Find out what's happening in their life and experience life together. Celebrate and congratulate them when achievements enter their life and pray for them when they face difficult times. A genuine concern and love for others will be a driving force that will set you a part in this life and establish your legacy.

There is a guy named David Sandler who published 49 rules called the Sandler rules. I like a good bit of what he wrote, and we both believe in several similar principles worded differently. With that stated, there is one Sandler's rule that rubs me completely wrong, *"the bottom line of sales is to make a sale and go to the bank, you're not in sales to make a friend."*

Really? How callous! Is it more important to sell at all costs? I adamantly disagree with this statement, and I find it to be the fundamental reason why prospective clients and customers think poorly of a salesperson. Selling under this philosophy is a selfish way to present a product or service in the trade of sales. When you become less concerned about the principles that make friends and are more focused on materialism, you have failed selling under the "golden rule".

The Sandler philosophy might work for a couple of years, and you might be the top salesperson for a season, but is it worth it? Does the pursuit of money outweigh the importance of building a meaningful relationship? Personally, I like to make a sale, but I want my client to have a good experience. I never want people to say, "All Scotti cares about is making the sale and going to the bank."

Once you build a bad reputation, it's hard to shake it off. Due to the Internet and social media, people can see what others think about you instantly and permanently. A reputation, good or bad, remains in the public eye for a lifetime. If potential customers hear that you and your company are nothing more than a "cold" insensitive company that is results driven, good luck with that "sales nugget" Mr. Sandler.

You want people to look forward to your visit and this happens when you treat others in a kind and respectful way. You want your friendship to last far longer than the income, trips, recognition, or fame you receive when you make a sale.

2

Time Is Important To Everyone

Let's look at the communication taking place in the world today. Other people are calling on your sales contact besides you. Your contact is plain busy. They still have their daily responsibilities to run their company besides their personal lives. Now we bring into the mix new technology that educates, entertains, and brings us daily solicitations, letters, emails, Internet ads, catalogs, flyers, phone messages, and television ads. It's a wonder you ever get an audience with a person to make a sales pitch.

Digital marketing experts at PPC Protect in February of 2021, stated that in the 1970's, the average person was exposed to 500 to 1600 adds per day. This was mostly through billboards, newspapers, and TV. In 2007 the marketing research firm Yankelovich estimated the average person saw up to 5,000 adds per day and it was described by the consumer as out of control. In 2021, the average person is exposed to between 6,000 and 10,000 adds per day. Digital advertising is driving the increase and an example is Google making $134 Billion in 2019, just on advertising.

Decision makers are getting bombarded, and sales techniques are wearing them out. Then you show up! Don't fret; it's all positive and an opportunity.

Taking all that into consideration, what can you do to not appear like an unwanted commercial interrupting their favorite show? First, ask them up front, "Is this a good time for you?" If not, set up another time to call them back. They usually respond, "What's this about?" It's right here that you need to deliver your best elevator speech in under a minute.

Be precise; hit the high points, be interesting, refreshing and have passion. Rather than try and close the deal immediately, just deliver a winning "hook". Then ask them, "May we set up another time to discuss more details when it's convenient for you?"

Several times in my sales career I'd be talking with someone, and you could sense it just wasn't the right time even though they'd agreed to the meeting. I'd say, "I want to apologize because I can tell that you have something else on your mind that's pressing and I'm visiting you at a bad time. Maybe we should reschedule to another day that will be a better time for you?"

Using this process, I've had all types of responses: "I

apologize, I have a lot going on at work" or "Something just came up this morning" or "No please go ahead, that's my fault" or "You know I am just not interested in this right now and I probably shouldn't have agreed to a meeting."

You can turn the lemons into lemonade if you can convince them to reschedule. Don't be afraid to get up and walk out if you sense they're in "la la land" during your meeting. Just ask to re-engage at a later date.

Even when I've scheduled an established time for a meeting, I still always begin, "We have scheduled an hour for our meeting today. Is that still good for you?" They will immediately let you know your time allotment and that will help you arrange your presentation accordingly. The worst thing you can do is to take more time than you've been granted. When you come to the end of your time, even if you haven't told your story, state, "I just noticed we are up against the clock right now, I want to be respectful of your time." If they give you more time, take it and run with it. If not, be respectful of their time, walk out and call on them another day.

3

Work Smart, Not Just Hard

WORKING SMART encompasses everything from proper prospecting, to learning and practicing good sales techniques. There are dozens of books on using your time wisely. Yet, one system doesn't fit everyone. Find out what sales method or technique delivers success, then repeat that system over and over, again and again.

In today's world, I think the best run college football program in the NCAA is the University of Alabama. Look at their results. They compete for a championship almost every year. They have a system that Coach Nick Saban has created that works, so they repeat the same routine over and over. They don't just work harder than everyone else. They also work smarter. Coach Saban has developed a successful system and he replicates that system over and over, every year, every month, every day, every hour, and every minute. He preaches to his players, "You can only control the moment in time right now so concentrate on every little step, one step at a time."

Find the success trail that works for you and repeat it over and over. If you are having good results, stay on the path that yields success. If your sales are suffering, find something that is working for someone else and try their path. Work smart by uncovering what works best for you.

4

People Throw Rocks From
The Back Of The Line Forward

IT IS GREAT TO ASPIRE to become exceptional in your sales career, but beware of the fallout. Success often breed's jealousy among the average achievers and some of your co-workers may be incredibly envious at your success. Sadly, some people are resentful of those that are more successful than themselves. You might be admired while also disliked for no other reason other than you are more successful than them. If you are a "super star" on your sales team, there's a good chance your closest friends may be outside of your work environment.

People who are jealous of others' success are just simple minded. They are short sighted in their views on life and don't realize that there is plenty of opportunity for success for everyone. They think only a few people are designated to be successful and spend more time envious of others that do well, than concentrating on how they, too, can be successful. On the flip side, be genuinely happy for other's success. You don't need a scarcity mentality, because there is plenty of room for many to be successful.

When I was working with Aflac, there was a six-year period when I was the top salesperson. Aflac had two national contests and recognition was based on total insurance premium produced during a set time. I was awarded the top award for six consecutive years: President of the National Convention and the Chairman of the President's Club. My premium numbers were ridiculous. I might have $30,000,000 in premium production and the next closest agent would have $1,500,000. Thanks to landing Wal-Mart, I had more individual production than most states and territories within Aflac, as well as every one of the 50,000 individual agents competing for the top award.

It wasn't long before I could sense the insincere congratulations coming from fellow associates. I'd see my peers at national conventions, and they would meet me and offer a congratulation that felt halfhearted. It became quite uncomfortable for me, and I could feel the resentment and the jealousy others felt towards my success. I would hear people whispering, "Boy is he lucky. I wish that were me." Never mind that I'd qualified for dozens of other conventions in a twenty-year career prior to Wal-Mart. To my critics, I was an overnight success only due to one large account, Wal-Mart. After being recognized as the best for six years in a row, and not just winning, but dominating, I contacted Aflac and told them to find a way to retire me and allow someone else the opportunity to win the top award going forward.

I felt like everyone standing in the back of the line was tossing rocks towards the back of my head. I allowed other's contempt towards my success to negatively affect my well-being. It was quite hurtful for me to be up on stage feeling the fog of envy in the room. Thankfully, Aflac came up with some other way to recognize me and they called it the "Chairman Emeritus of Aflac Award". Imagine Nick Saban calling the SEC commissioner and saying, "I know we had an undefeated season and won the SEC championship, but I think we will sit out the presentation, so go ahead and award the runner-up team first place." That should never happen.

As soon as I became Chairman Emeritus and everyone else had a chance to take home the first-place hardware, people acted nicer to me. The Aflac sales force were once again happy being able to compete for the number one spot. Even though in reality they were still second best, the perception of winning first place changed the atmosphere. Maybe that's why today "everyone gets a trophy", so more people appear happy.

Let's again look at some more of Marcus Aurelius' words … a man that understood pain like few of us ever will. The famous emperor of Rome writes how to overcome the pettiness of people, "*When you wake up in the morning tell yourself, the people I deal with today will be meddling, ungrateful, arrogant, dishonest, jealous and surly."* Marcus appropriately described everyone jealous in the back of the line. You think he gave everyone a trophy in the Roman army?

Handle your success with deep humility and be aware of how some people may treat you unkindly if you happen to win all the time. Learn to take it with a grain of salt. Learn to shake it off and keep on striving for perfection. I still think it's far better to win, to be in the front of the line … even if the back of your head hurts from rocks tossed towards the front.

5

Why Wait Until Tomorrow To Do What Can Be Done Today?

Too many times I witness people "putting off" something they can accomplish today to a time somewhere in the future. For example, maybe you tell yourself, I'm going to write some thank you notes or a sympathy card this Friday. All day Friday will be my day to catch up on notes and paperwork. Well, under first impression it appears to be a good plan considering it's three days away. Yet today some time unexpectantly became available to accomplish the task of writing notes, yet you choose to indulge in some R and R or just chill the rest of the day. Friday rolls around and an emergency occurs; your child is sick; your in-laws are in the hospital; a friend's car breaks down; your teenager gets in trouble at school. Something comes up unexpected! There is no time for paperwork.

You get the picture. Too many times I see good intentions, well thought out future plans to accomplish a simple task interrupted so that a worthy goal in the future goes unaccomplished. If there is time left in today and you have a window of time where something can be accomplished that you are putting off for the future, just do it. Complete your task today for we do not have the guarantee of tomorrow.

6

A Warm Sales Door Is Easier To Open

REFERRALS ARE IMPORTANT to a successful career in sales. You will quickly learn that there are "cold doors" and there are "warm doors". A "cold door" is nothing more than a "cold call", which you will experience with some success. A "warm door" is when someone with whom you have either a friendship or a current business relationship introduces you to another "opportunity sale" that is actually their close relationship. It is a very powerful way to fast track your sales success.

I strongly believe that you need to earn your referrals to take advantage of "warm doors". Let me explain. If you have done a good job for a customer, provided a quality product or service and delivered exactly what you promised, then you've earned the right to ask for a referral. When you ask for a referral at the beginning of a business relationship, it's far too early. You should allow time to determine if you, your company, or your products delivered the complete satisfaction you're selling.

Most of the time people don't like to be the first to try something out. They would rather someone else be the "beta test" for the latest and greatest in the market. A person likes for the kinks to be worked out and then buy something already proven. They would rather be the second one to use a proven product. It's OK if it's early in the development of a product for they might trade for better terms and put up with some early growth problems. It's important that your customer is completely satisfied first before ever asking for their referral. You owe it your client first and foremost, to do your job and deliver on your promises before asking them to put their reputation on the line for your sales career.

You might not think it's that big a deal to ask someone, "Hey I could really use a favor. Would you mind recommending me to some of your friends, so I can talk to them about the same thing I'm doing for you?" Reflect for a moment, do you like to recommend something or someone to another friend or business relationship when it's new and unproven? Probably not! Without a proven product or service, you're asking this person to help you sell something they themselves have not seen be of benefit at this point in the business relationship. It's very unprofessional to ask someone to stake his or her reputation on an unproven product or "widget". Do a good job first and allow time for your company to perform admirably. When you have earned it, then, ask for that "warm door" favor.

7

Learn To Enjoy What You Do From An Internal Perspective

Can receiving praise in excess actually make you less successful? That is an interesting question that I would like to address.

First, I'm all for positive motivation and letting people know they are valuable ... in a healthy way. It was nice to hear I played well. But as in all things, even too much praise, is not a good thing. The so-called self-esteem movement in the 1980's and 90's would have you believe that you can never have enough positive reinforcement. If a little praise is good, then a lot is even better.

As theory's would like you to believe, raising someone's self-esteem all the time will help them perform better, be smarter, persuade us to sobriety, etc. ... That's like saying if one headache tablet gets rid of a migraine, then a bottle of tablets will certainly make you feel even better. I believe you can become addicted to an unhealthy dosage of outward praise.

There are many studies on this topic but one in particular was a study published in 1998 in the Journal of Personality and Social Psychology. Children were rewarded for "just doing their own thing" – drawing, playing, just being a kid. When the rewards of praise were eventually discontinued in the trial, the children lost interest in normal activities. They went from being satisfied with the intrinsic reward (the enjoyment of doing an activity for its own sake) to contingent reward – (doing the activity for the sake of an external reward). A contingent reward in excess reduces the appeal of an intrinsic reward. The children stopped seeking satisfaction from the activity, doing something they should be doing anyway and started expecting satisfaction from a source outside the activity, such as praise from an adult.

So, how can we apply this to sales? Learn to accept external praise with a humble spirit. Yet, expecting constant praise from what should be everyday habits of improving the "walk and the talk", (charismatic, passionate, innovative, driven, responsible, caring, helpful, outgoing, poised, attentive, knowledgeable, funny, focused, good listener, self-directed, goal oriented, good communicator, self-starter, quick-witted, well informed, and trustworthy) can diminish genuine internal motivation. We don't want these attributes to be the exception; we want them to be the norm in your daily life and your value, purpose and satisfaction comes from the intrinsic value of just trying to be "exceptional" in all areas with people. Thrive on the internal self-satisfaction of giving it your best rather than seeking the outward praise to perform.

8

If You Toss Enough Footballs, Somebody Will Eventually Stand Up And Catch One

THE MORE QUALITY calls you make, the more sales you will close. It becomes a game of numbers. You will get more "no's" than a "yes". If I had to guess, you probably have three wins for every seven losses. If you want 3 people to buy, then you need to pitch your product to 10 prospects. Even after you have everything right on the front end ... a good product, proper preparation, well groomed, a solid prepared presentation and a commitment to quality service, you will still hear "no" often.

As the story goes, I didn't see much playing time at quarterback for Vanderbilt. There's only so much that a good coach can do with limited talent. Even if I had played a lot, it wouldn't have made a whole lot of difference during my three years of SEC football. We were 2 - 9 each season, 2 being wins. If Peyton Manning had been our starting quarterback, we probably wouldn't have been much better.

When the head coach called me off the bench, "get ready

to go in, go warm up", I would scramble to find receivers to warm up with me. Oddly, it was one of the student equipment managers that first stepped up to catch my passes preparing me to enter the game. The student equipment manager who always stepped up was Steve R. Dozier, now a Criminal Court Judge in Nashville, TN.

Steve enjoys telling the story, "I would see Scotti search frantically for a football to throw. I'd get him a ball and start playing catch with him. If Scotti tossed enough footballs with me, eventually another receiver might stand up, take my place, and start catching his passes."

So, in sales if you toss enough presentations someone will eventually say "yes" and catch one. You have no control over the many variables affecting the decision maker. Negative circumstances may affect their ability to listen. Maybe they had a bad day at home or something chaotic happened at work or there is trouble with a co-worker. The importance of large numbers is that you create some stability in your sales success. The law of large numbers (lots of presentations) guarantees stable long-term results that offset random negative events. If you have a quota to meet every month, the way to successfully hit your numbers is to back into that number. Closing three sales means ten or more presentations to hit that number. Sometimes you might experience less than three out of ten wins. The next ten presentations you might close four to five sales. It all averages out. Start tossing the football as many times as you can!

9

When You're Wrong, Just Go Ahead And Fall On The Sword

IF A CUSTOMER CALLS you out and you messed up, don't start making excuses. Sometimes you may have to "eat a little crow" or "Blue Jay", even when it's not your fault. Own up to your mistake and just "fall on the sword", i.e., "Sir, I'm very sorry I haven't met your expectations and I'm here to make it right."

Isn't the problem rectified when you go to a restaurant and they totally mess up the meal and the manager comes back to your table, apologizes, and comps your meal, or gives you free desert or a gift certificate? The manager is falling on the sword and attempting to keep you as a satisfied customer. Retaining an at-risk customer is much more economical than finding new business.

If your client continues to vent on you about a certain mistake, accept his/her concerns biting your lip if necessary. Remember it's probably not personal and even if it is personal and you're the culprit of bad service or irresponsibility, just agree with the customer and make it right. It never serves you well acting defensive because your customer is your customer. You need to give them the floor and the benefit of doubt.

You might find out through proper dialogue that your client is looked upon badly based on something you didn't deliver. Or they might have a family problem; something is blowing up in their marriage or maybe they have a wayward child. You just happen to be the "dog" they need to kick in order to get some relief in their life.

During those uncomfortable moments I used to say, "Is there anything else you'd like to say to me?" I'd listen until they were finished and then ask. "Is there any more you would like to cover? How can we make it right?" Sooner than later, you will get to the root of the problem.

Always offer to make it right and then do everything you can to diffuse the situation. Instead of focusing on the hostility, look to a solution and the best way to move forward. The road to an amicable solution always begins first when someone displays humility and admits they're wrong, so be the first, do right, and just "fall on the sword."

10

Performance Enhancing Devices—PED's

IN THE PAST FORTY YEARS, the sale's tools to improve your closing ratio have grown a 100-fold. When I first started selling, I used a notebook and an annual calendar to hand write and record my daily activities, so I could plan my weeks and months to be more productive. Later, someone came out with a Day-Timer Planner which was an enhanced improvement on managing your time. You could buy a small handheld notebook and work with either a 1-page-per-day planner or a 2-page-per-day planner. It was pitched as a product to help busy people organize their lives. It was a game changer for me. I could plan and conquer and then find in the notes where I'd been and where I needed to go, working much more efficiently.

Then in the 80's someone came up with a pager or affectionally known as a beeper. I worked even more effectively because someone could send me a page/text message and I could respond quicker to my clients. It soon became my two-way method of communication sending and receiving SMS messages. Then the cell phone was created, and even more efficiencies were created through technology.

I remember the time I was playing golf at Callaway Gardens in Georgia with a prospective client from California. I was sitting in a cart with him, and he told me he was going to check his email. I expected to see him leave the course and head back to his room. To my surprise, he whipped out this handheld device called a Blackberry and I watched him send an email and then hit his golf ball, and he never left the tee box. I thought, "That's incredible. I can be even more efficient." So, the next week I bought a Blackberry. Each time better technology was introduced in the business world, I jumped on board in an effort to maintain a competitive edge.

Look at what you have at your fingertips today just within a cell phone with emails; calendars; contacts list; to to-do lists; documents; phone calling; text messages, to the ability to deliver presentations. Between Apple and Samsung alone, you can remain on the cutting edge. Still there are other tools that operate on your phone to improve your game. I call them performance enhancing devices - PED's.

When I played baseball in the late 80's performance enhancing drugs or PED's started becoming newsworthy. You had the "bash brothers" in Jose Conseco and Mark McGwire at Oakland that were not only hitting lots of homeruns, but the baseball was traveling record distances. Then in 1998 you had the chase at Roger Maris' home run record of 61 between Mark McGwire of St. Louis Cardinals, Ken Griffey of the Seattle Mariners, and Sammy Sosa of the Chicago Cubs. Two of those players eclipsed the record when McGwire hit 70 homeruns and Sosa hit 66. Their exploits were later tainted due to their admittance of using PED's.

People have always searched for the performance enhancing "whatever's" to be the best they can be. The first person to actually seek a chemical advantage in baseball was Pud Galvin way back in 1889. His performance-enhancing substance was a testosterone supplement derived from the testicles of live animals such as dogs and guinea pigs. Now Pud was a guy who really wanted to win.

In order to improve your "walk and talk", you don't need a chemical substance made from the testicles of animals to improve your performance. To be the very best you can be, you need to use PED's, not "performance enhancing drugs", but rather "performance enhancing devices" that are readily available today.

By the time you read this, something else has come along and replaced the latest and greatest mentioned yesterday. Have a thirst for streamlining your sales process and continuously look for PED's in sales improvement technology that can give you a competitive edge.

CPSIA information can be obtained
at www.ICGtesting.com
Printed in the USA
LVHW081627270922
729403LV00025B/237